剑桥教育文选

〔英〕A. C. 本森 主编

辜 涛 译

CAMBRIDGE
ESSAYS
ON
EDUCATION

社会科学文献出版社
SOCIAL SCIENCES ACADEMIC PRESS (CHINA)

图书在版编目（CIP）数据

剑桥教育文选＝Cambridge essays on education：英文／（英）
本森（Benson, A.C.）主编；辜涛译.—北京：社会科学文献出版社，
2014.8
　ISBN 978-7-5097-6193-9

　Ⅰ.①剑…　Ⅱ.①本…　②辜…　Ⅲ.①教育－文集－英文
Ⅳ.①G4-53

　中国版本图书馆 CIP 数据核字（2014）第 141817 号

剑桥教育文选
————————

主　　编／〔英〕A.C. 本森
译　　者／辜　涛

出 版 人／谢寿光
出 版 者／社会科学文献出版社
地　　址／北京市西城区北三环中路甲 29 号院 3 号楼华龙大厦
邮政编码／100029

责任部门／社会政法分社（010）59367156　　　责任编辑／张建中　芮素平
电子信箱／shekebu@ssap.cn　　　　　　　　　责任校对／安瑞匣
项目统筹／芮素平　　　　　　　　　　　　　　责任印制／岳　阳
经　　销／社会科学文献出版社市场营销中心（010）59367081　59367089
读者服务／读者服务中心（010）59367028

印　　装／三河市尚艺印装有限公司
开　　本／787mm×1092mm　1/16　　　　　　印　　张／11
版　　次／2014 年 8 月第 1 版　　　　　　　　字　　数／163 千字
印　　次／2014 年 8 月第 1 次印刷
书　　号／ISBN 978-7-5097-6193-9
定　　价／39.00 元

西华师范大学资助
西华师范大学中国文学文化译介研究中心资助

PREFACE

The scheme of publishing a volume of essays dealing with underlying aims and principles of education was originated by the University Press Syndicate. It seemed to promise something both of use and interest, and the further arrangements were entrusted to a small Committee, with myself as secretary and acting editor.

Our idea has been this: at a time of much educational enterprise and unrest, we believed that it would be advisable to collect the opinions of a few experienced teachers and administrators upon certain questions of the theory and motive of education which lie a little beneath the surface.

To deal with current and practical problems does not seem the *first* need at present. Just now, work is both common as well as fashionable; most people are doing their best; and, if anything, the danger is that organisation should outrun foresight and intelligence. Moreover a weakening of the old compulsion of the classics has resulted, not in perfect freedom, but in a tendency on the part of some scientific enthusiasts simply to substitute compulsory science for compulsory literature, when the real question rather is whether obligatory subjects should not be diminished as far as possible, and more sympathetic attention given to faculty and aptitude.

We have attempted to avoid mere current controversial topics, and to encourage our contributors to define as far as possible the aim and outlook of education, as the word is now interpreted.

We have not furthered any educational conspiracy, nor attempted any fusion of view. Our plan has been first to select some of the most pressing of modern problems,

前　言

　　出版一本论文集讨论教育的深层目的和原则，这个计划首先由剑桥大学出版社理事会提出来。这个计划看起来既有益又有趣，所以接下来的工作就委托给了一个编辑委员会落实，由我担任该委员会的秘书和执行编辑。

　　我们的想法是：在当前这样一个时代，大家对教育的发展既满怀信心又忐忑不安，如果我们能收集一些富有经验的教师和教育管理者在教育理论和教育目标方面对某些问题比较深刻的见解，应该是大有裨益的。

　　目前，应付当前的实际问题似乎并非第一要务。在当前社会，人们外出工作司空见惯；绝大多数人正全力以赴想要做到最好；如果社会中有什么让人担心的话，也不过是组织机构应该更有远见和智慧。而且，人们对古典文学的传统爱好越来越弱，结果带来的并非完全的自由，而是另外一种倾向，就是那些热爱科学的狂热分子想要简单地用理科必修课来代替文学必修课。事实上，教育中真正的问题其实在于我们是否应该尽量保持现有的必修课程；是否应该把更多的注意力放在教师的能力和学生的天赋上。

　　我们尽量避免挑选当前有争议的主题，并鼓励撰稿人尽量深入地探讨教育的目的和前景。

　　我们不旨在推动任何教育计划的落实，也不尝试融

next to find well-equipped experts and students to deal with each, and then to give the various writers as free a hand as possible, desiring them to speak with the utmost frankness and personal candour. We have not directed the plan or treatment or scope of any essay; and my own editorial supervision has consisted merely in making detailed suggestions on smaller points, in exhorting contributors to be punctual and diligent, and generally revising what the New Testament calls jots and tittles. We have been very fortunate in meeting with but few refusals, and our contributors readily responded to the wish which we expressed, that they should write from the personal rather than from the judicial point of view, and follow their own chosen method of treatment.

We take the opportunity of expressing our obligations to all who have helped us, and to Viscount Bryce for bestowing, as few are so justly entitled to do, an educational benediction upon our scheme and volume.

A.C. BENSON

MAGDALENE COLLEGE, CAMBRIDGE

August 18, 1917

合任何教育观点。我们的计划是首先挑选出现在最迫切的问题，然后找到最具能力的专家和学者来解答这些问题，最后为每个作者提供尽可能大的自由，希望他们能在文章中以最坦诚和直率的态度表达意见。我们对任何一篇文章都没有限定其写作计划、写作方式和范围，我个人的编辑职责也仅限于在一些小的方面提出具体建议，敦促撰稿人勤奋写作、准时交稿，修改的地方仅限于《圣经·新约》所说的"细微之处"。幸运的是，几乎没有作者拒绝我们，他们都积极回应我们的计划，表示在写作方式上会遵从个人的想法，而非那些正统的观念。

借此机会，我谨向所提供帮助的人表示感谢，特别要感谢布莱斯子爵，让我们有机会实现计划，出版这本教育文选。

A. C. 本森
剑桥大学莫德林学院
1917 年 8 月 18 日

CONTENTS

目　　录

理想的教育应当把一切和美联系起来……把一切和伟大的艺术形式以及高尚的思想与行为联系起来。

——W·百特森

THE PLACE OF SCIENCE IN EDUCATION

By W. BATESON
Director of the John Innes Horticultural Institution [①]

That secondary education in England fails to do what it might is scarcely in dispute. The magnitude of the failure will be appreciated by those who know what other countries accomplish at a fraction of the cost. Beyond the admission that something is seriously wrong there is little agreement. We are told that the curriculum is too exclusively classical, that the classes are too large, the teaching too dull, the boys too much away from home, the examination-system too oppressive, athletics overdone. All these things are probably true. Each cause contributes in its degree to the lamentable result. Yet, as it seems to me, we may remove them all without making any great improvement. All the circumstances may be varied, but that intellectual apathy which has become so marked a characteristic of English life, especially of English public and social life, may not improbably continue. Why nations pass into these morbid phases no one can tell. The spirit of the age, that "polarisation of society" as Tarde [②] used to call it, in a definite direction, is brought about by no cause that can

---

① The John Innes Horticultural Institution (John Innes Centre): 英国约翰·英纳斯研究所, 也称 "约翰·英纳斯中心", 是英国最优秀的基因科学和植物研究中心, 也是世界上顶尖的研究所之一。中心始建于 1910 年, 由地产商和慈善家约翰·英纳斯捐款建立。在过去的一百年间, 英纳斯家族为科学做出了巨大的贡献。如今该研究所成为英国农业不可或缺的支柱之一。自 20 世纪 80 年代以来, 约翰·英纳斯中心已经为中国培养了百余名植物分子生物学界高端人才。

② Tarde: 此处可能是指 Jean-Gabriel De Tarde (1843~1904), 法国社会学家、犯罪学家和社会心理学家, 他认为社会学是以个体间的心理相互作用为基础的, 其基础的动力是模仿和创新。

论科学在教育中的地位

W. 百特森

约翰·英纳斯研究所主任

很少有人讨论英国的中学教育缺失了什么。只有那些了解其他国家付出了什么代价、取得了什么成就的人士，才清楚这种缺失的严重程度。大家都承认中学教育肯定出了严重问题，但除此之外，就众说纷纭。有人说，教学大纲太偏重古典文学，以至于有些独断；有人说班级太大；有人说教学很枯燥；有人说学生离家太远；有人说考试压力太大；还有人说体育课太过头，等等。所有这些都有可能是真的。每一个因素都不同程度地导致了现在的可悲结果。但是，我认为，即使解决了以上所有问题，我们的教育也不会有太大的进步。实际情况可能有所不同，但英国公众和英国社会对知识的冷漠，已经根深蒂固为一种国民性格，并且还在延续。为什么一个民族会发展到这种病态的阶段？没有人知道。这个时代的精神，用塔德曾经说过的话来描述，就是在某个确定方向上"社会的两极分化"，其原因我们现在还说不清楚。除非我们能真正洞察英国社会心理，否则这种特征还会继续下去，不受我们的意志控制。一般英国人对教育、知识和学习的态度基本上是一窝蜂地模仿。在所有的模仿行为中，总有这么

be named as yet. It will remain beyond volitional control at least until we get some real insight into social physiology. That the attitude or pose of the average Englishman towards education, knowledge, and learning is largely a phenomenon of infectious imitation we know. But even if we could name the original, perhaps real, perhaps fictional, person—for in all likelihood there was such an one—whom English society in its folly unconsciously selected as a model, the knowledge would advance us little. The psychology of imitation is still impenetrable and likely to remain so. The simple interpretation of our troubles as a form of sloth—a travelling along lines of least resistance—can scarcely be maintained. For first there have been times when learning and science were the fashion. Whether society benefited directly therefrom may, in passing, be doubted, but certainly learning did. Secondly there are plenty of men who under the pressure of fashion devote much effort to the improvement of their form in fatuous sports, which otherwise applied would go a considerable way in the improvement of their minds and in widening their range of interests.

Of late things have become worse. In the middle of the nineteenth century a perfunctory and superficial acquaintance with recent scientific discovery was not unusual among the upper classes, and the scientific world was occasionally visited even by the august. These slender connections have long since withered away. This decline in the public estimation of science and scientific men has coincided with a great increase both in the number of scientific students and in the provision for teaching science. It has occurred also in the period during which something of the full splendour and power of science has begun to be revealed. Great regions of knowledge have been penetrated by the human mind. The powers of man over nature have been multiplied a hundredfold. The fate of nations hangs literally on the issue of contemporary experiments in the laboratory; but those who govern the Empire are quite content to know nothing of all this. Intercommunication between government departments and scientific advisers has of course much developed. That, even in this country, was inevitable. Otherwise the Empire might have collapsed long since. Experts in the sciences are from time to time invited to confer with heads of Departments and even Cabinet Ministers, explaining to them, as best they may, the rudiments of their respective studies, but such occasional night-school talks to the great are an inadequate recognition of the position of science in a modern State.

一个原型，但是，即使我们能找出整个英国社会这种愚蠢的模仿行为中，被无意识地树立为榜样去模仿的那个人——不管是真实的还是虚构的，对我们意义也不大。模仿心理仍然牢不可破，并将继续下去。如果把我们的麻烦简单地解释为树懒式的生活、一种阻力最小的生活，似乎也说不通。因为，第一，在英国的某些时期，学习和科学是一种潮流，整个社会是否从中受益，可能难以确定，但学习本身肯定从这种潮流中受益匪浅；第二，很多人，基于潮流的压力，下大力气通过很多愚蠢的运动来改善他们的体形，这些力气，如果用在其他方面，很可能会改善他们的心智，拓宽他们的兴趣范围。

近来，情况变得更为糟糕。在19世纪中期，上层阶级开始对最新的科学发现有了肤浅且似是而非的了解，甚至时不时拜访科学界人士。这种联系很久没有出现过了。虽然理科学生的人数和理科教学经费都在不断上升，但公众对科学和科学界人士的评价则在不断下降。在科学刚刚显露出其光辉与力量的时期，这种现象也出现过。但人类已经打破了对知识的迷信。毫不夸张地说，民族的命运掌握在实验室里那些最新的实验之中，可惜那些掌控帝国的人对此一无所知，而且对这种现状甚为满意。好在政府部门和科学顾问之间的联系大大加强了，这在当今形势下是不可避免的，否则帝国早就衰落了。科学家们常常会应邀和各部门首脑甚至内阁大臣商谈，尽最大的努力向他们阐释各自研究的基础内容。但是，在一个现代国家中，这种夜校式的断断续续的探讨其实显示了人们对科学的地位认识不足。科学不是一种随意在角落里撒一点就够了的物质，而是拟订每一项行动计划、制定每一条政策必须依赖的、永恒而不可或缺的指路明灯。

Science is not a material to be bought round the corner by the dram, but the one permanent and indispensable light in which every action and every policy must be judged.

To scientific men this is so evident that they are unable to imagine what the world looks like to other people. They cannot realise that by a majority of even the educated classes the phenomena of nature and the affairs of mankind are still seen through the old screens of mystery and superstition. The man of science regards nature as in great and ever increasing measure a soluble problem. For the layman such inquiries are either indifferent and somewhat absurd, or, if they attract his attention at all, are interesting only as possible sources of profit. I suspect that the distinction between these two classes of mind is not to any great degree a product of education.

It is contemporary commonplace that if science were more prominent in our educational system everybody would learn it and things would come all right. That interest in science would be extended is probable. There is in the population a residuum of which we will speak later, who would profit by the opportunity; but that the congenitally unscientific, the section from which the heads of government temporal and spiritual, the lawyers, administrators, politicians, the classes upon whose minds the public life of this country almost wholly depends, would by imbibition of scientific diet at any period of life, however early, be essentially altered seems in a high degree unlikely. Of the converse case we have long experience, and I would ask those who entertain such sanguine expectations, whether the results of administering literature to scientific boys give much encouragement to their views. This consideration brings us to the one hard, physiological fact that should form the foundation of all educational schemes: the congenital diversity of the individual types. Education has too long been regarded as a kind of cookery: put in such and such ingredients in given proportions and a definite product will emerge. But living things have not the uniformity which this theory of education assumes. Our population is a medley of many kinds which will continue heterogeneous, to whatever system of education they are submitted, just as various types of animals maintain their several characteristics though nourished on identical food, or as you may see various sorts of apples remaining perfectly distinct though grafted on the same stock. Their diversity is congenital.

According to the proposal of the reformers the natural sciences should be

对于研究科学的人来说，这个道理是显而易见的，以至于他们不能想象其他人是怎么看待这个世界的。他们没有想到，大部分人，甚至是受过教育的阶层，仍然用神秘和迷信的眼光看待自然和人类社会的现象。科学界人士认为，以一种不断进步的方式征服自然是可行的，而其他人，对探究自然则漠不关心，甚至觉得荒谬；如果他们最终对这方面产生了兴趣，不过是因为这可能成为另一个利益来源而已。我认为这两种心理的差异多多少少可以看作教育的产物。

目前大家公认，如果理科在我们的教育体系中地位更重要的话，每个人都愿意学习理科，事情就好办多了。人们对科学的兴趣会更大。肯定会有一小撮社会渣滓乘机从中牟利，这个我们以后再说。这样的话，这个国家公共生活所完全依赖的政府的世俗和精神领袖，以及律师、管理层、政客等，早晚都会在生活中受到科学的影响，从而发生根本性的变化，那么他们几乎与生俱来的非科学性也会得到极大改善。其实对于相反的情形，我们倒是有长期的经验，所以我想问问那些抱有乐观希望的人，是否向理科学生教授文学的现实在很大程度上支持了他们的这种观点。这种考虑促使我们注意到一个确定无疑的生理学方面的事实，这个事实应该是所有教育计划的基础：不同个体具有与生俱来的多样性。长期以来，教育被认为像一种烹饪艺术：以固定比例加入这种或者那种原料，就可以烹饪出某种菜肴。但生物并不具有这种教育理论所假设的基础。人类有各种不同的类型，不管接受哪种教育，这种不同都会继续下去，就像不同的动物，吃同样的食物，还是会保持不同的特性；就像不同种类的苹果，就算嫁接到相同的树上，还是会长得完全不同。这种不同是天生的。

universally taught and be given "capital importance" in the examinations for the government services, but, cordially as we may approve the suggestion, we ought to consider what exactly its adoption is likely to effect. The intention of the proposal is doubtless that our public servants, especially the highest of them, shall, while preserving the great qualities they now possess, add also a knowledge of science and especially scientific habits of mind. Such is the "ample proposition that hope makes." [1] Does experience of men accord with it at all? Education, whether we like it or not, is a selective agency. I doubt whether the change proposed will sensibly alter the characters of the group on whom our choice at present falls. Rather, if forced upon an unwilling community, must it act by substituting another group. The most probable result would not be that the type of men who now fill great positions would become scientific, but rather that their places would be taken by men of an altogether distinct mental type. At the present time these two types of men meet but little. They scarcely know each other. Their differences are profound, affecting thoughts, ways of looking at things, and mental interests of every kind. If either could for a moment see the world with the vision of the other he would be amazed, but to do so he would need at least to be born again, and probably, as Samuel Butler [2] remarked, of different parents. No doubt the abler man of either type could learn with more or less effort or unreadiness the subject-matter and principles of the other's business, but any one who has watched the habits of the two classes will perceive that for them in any real sense to exchange interests, or that either should adopt the scheme of proportion which the other assigns to the events of nature and of life, a metamorphosis well nigh miraculous must be presupposed.

The Bishop of London speaking lately on behalf of the National Mission said that nature helped him to believe in God, and as evidence for his belief referred to the fact that we are not "blown off" this earth as it rushes through space, declaring that this

---

[1]　"ample proposition that hope makes"："希望所衍生出的提议"，源自莎士比亚戏剧《特洛埃勒斯与克雷雪达》(Troilus and Cressida)。

[2]　Samuel Butler：塞缪尔·巴特勒（1835~1902），英国维多利亚时代的反传统作家，发表了多种作品，最著名的两部作品包括乌托邦讽刺文《埃瑞璜》及其死后出版的半自传体小说《众生之路》。巴特勒同时还以对东正教的批判，对进化论的独立研究，对意大利艺术、文学、历史的研究而出名。另外，其翻译作品《伊利亚特》和《奥德赛》至今仍在使用。

有些改革者提议，自然科学应该在学校广泛教授，同时为了更好地为政府服务，自然科学在考试中也应该占有重要地位。但是，我们既然真心同意这个建议，就应该仔细考虑如何将其落到实处。毫无疑问，这个建议指向的是我们的公务员，尤其是高层，认为他们应该保持现有的高素质，同时具有科学知识尤其是科学的思维习惯。这就是"希望所衍生出的提议"。人们的经验是否也和这个提议相符呢？教育部门，无论我们喜欢与否，都是一个选择性的机构。我怀疑这个提议所带来的变化是否会理智地改变我们的选择所指向的群体。或者说，强迫这个群体接受他们不愿意的提议，他们可能会找其他群体代替自己。最可能的结果是，不是现在这群身居高位的人变得更有科学头脑，而是另外一群拥有完全不同头脑的人代替他们。目前这两种人差异很大，相互知之甚少，他们有不同的思维习惯，看待事物的方法和兴趣爱好也完全不同。如果他们肯用对方的视角观察这个世界，哪怕持有这种态度非常短暂，他们也会大为惊讶；但这样做对他们来说是完全不可能的，用塞缪尔·巴特勒的话来说，这样做的前提是他们在不同的父母孕育下，重生一次。毫无疑问，这两个群体中能干的人或多或少，或者是在无意识的情况下，会了解对方的处事原则和主要生活内容，但是任何一个人，只要观察了两个阶层的习惯，就会发现，对他们来说，要在真正意义上改变他们的兴趣、让其采纳对方看待自然界和生命的方式，几乎是不可能的。

伦敦主教最近代表全国教会组织说，是自然让他信奉上帝，这种信仰的证据源自下面的事实：地球在太空中飞速运行的时候，我们没有从地球上被"扫走"，这就证明"某个人"把 70 英里厚的空气包围在地球上，消除了这个灾难。有没有人认为，主教的这个口误其实想在

catastrophe had been averted because "Some one" had wrapped seventy miles of atmosphere round our planet. Does any one think that the Bishop's slip was in fact due to want of scientific teaching at Marlborough? His chances of knowing about Sir Isaac Newton, etc., have been as good as those of many familiar with the accepted version. I would rather suppose that such sublunary problems had not interested him in the least, and that he no more cared how we happen to stick on the earth's surface than St Paul cared how a grain of wheat or any other seed germinates beneath it, when he similarly was betrayed into an unfortunate illustration.

So too on the famous occasion—always cited in these debates—when a Home Secretary defended the Government for having permitted the importation of fats into Germany on the ground that the discovery that glycerine could be made from fat was a recent advance in chemistry [①] , he was not showing the defects of a literary education so much as a want of interest in the problems of nature, and the subject-matter of science at large. It is to be presumed indeed that neither fats, nor glycerine, nor the dependent problem how living bodies are related to the world they inhabit, had ever before seemed to him interesting. Nor can we suppose they would, even if chemistry were substituted for Greek in Responsions.

The difficulty in obtaining full recognition for science lies deeper than this. It is a part of public opinion or taste which may well survive changes in the educational system. Blunders about science like those illustrated above are soon excused. Few think much the worse of the perpetrators, whereas a corresponding obliviousness to language, history, literature, and indeed to learning other than their own which we of the scientific fraternity have agreed to condone in our members is incompatible with public life of a high order. Both classes have their disabilities. That of the scientific side is well expressed in an incident which befell the late Professor Hales.

---

① glycerine：甘油，是一种无色或微黄色透明黏稠液体，无毒、无臭、无腐蚀性，具有较强的吸湿性，可与有机酸和无机酸反应生成多种酯类。因为无论动物油脂还是植物油脂都是脂肪酸甘油三酯，在水解的过程中都可以得到甘油。甘油在 1779 年由斯柴尔（Scheel）首先发现，1823 年人们认识到油脂成分中含有 Chevreul（希腊语为"甘甜"的意思），因此命名为甘油（Glycerine），所以这不是最新的化学进展。此处作者是想讽刺那些官员在科学方面的无知。

马博罗推广科学教育？很多人熟悉万有引力理论，主教和这些人一样，有许多机会了解牛顿。我宁愿相信，这类问题丝毫不能引起他的兴趣，他从来没有想过我们为什么会附着在地球的表面，就像圣保罗因为从来没有关注过一粒麦子或者其他种子是如何发芽的，所以会相信错误的解释一样。

另外一个著名的例子在这类辩论中经常引用：一个内政部部长为政府辩论说，之所以允许向德国出口脂肪，是因为化学上一个新进展发现甘油可以用脂肪来制造。他并不是要表露出文科教育的缺陷乃至对自然问题和科学主题的兴趣。我们可以假设，不是脂肪，不是甘油，也不是生物和它们生存环境之间相互影响的问题，勾起了他的兴趣。即使化学课被希腊语课代替了，恐怕也不会勾起这类人的兴趣。

充分认识科学比这要困难得多。这种认识是公众舆论或者说审美的一部分，延续的时间肯定远远超过教育体系变化的时间。如上所述的科学性错误很快就会被大家原谅，很少有人会觉得犯错者有多么糟糕，相反，如果学习科学的人在语言、历史、文学或者他们自己学科以外的任何一门学科上犯了同样的错误，那么我们觉得这是可以理解的，但公众可能会觉得不可原谅。两个阶层都有各自的不足。科学阶层的弱点在已故黑尔斯教授的"事件"中已得到充分说明。在口语测试的时候，他指着一部希腊戏剧中的几行，问一个考生，想到了莎士比亚作品的哪一部分，这位考生回答："别这样，先生，我是学数学的。"而有些人，毫无疑问，宁愿不知道万有引力。比如，有人听说（就像我不久前一样），几个极诚实的理科学生，说他们记不起任何有关亚拿尼亚或者撒非喇的东西，另一个更有见识的说，虽然说不出理由，但他确信亚拿尼亚是一个骗子的名字。不得不承

Examining in the Little-Go *viva voce*, he asked a candidate, with reference to some line in a Greek play, what passage in Shakespeare it recalled to him, and received the answer "Please, sir, I am a mathematical man." Some, no doubt, would rather ignore gravitation. When, for example, one hears, as I did not long since, several scientific students own in perfect sincerity that they could not recall anything about Ananias and Sapphira [①] and another, more enlightened, say that he was sure Ananias was a name for a liar though he could not tell why, one is driven to admit that ignorance of this special but not uncommon kind does imply more than inability to remember an old legend. We may be reluctant to confess the fact, but though most scientific men have some recreation, often even artistic in nature, we have with rare exceptions withdrawn from the world in which letters, history and the arts have immediate value, and simple allusions to these topics find us wanting. Of the two kinds of disability which is the more grave? Truly gross ignorance of science darkens more of a man's mental horizon, and in its possible bearing on the destinies of a race is far more dangerous than even total blindness to the course of human history and endeavour; and yet it is difficult to question the popular verdict that to know nothing of gravitation though ridiculous is venial, while to know nothing of Ananias is an offence which can never be forgiven.

That is the real difficulty. The people of this country have definitely preferred the unscientific type, holding the other virtually in contempt. Their choice may be right or wrong, but that it is reversible seems unlikely. Such revolutions in public opinion are rare events. Democracy moreover inevitably worships and is swayed by the spoken word. As inevitably, the range and purposes of science daily more and more transcend the comprehension—even the educated comprehension—of the vulgar, who will of course elevate the nimble and versatile, speaking a familiar language, above dull and inarticulate natural philosophers.

In these discussions there is a disposition to forget how very largely natural science is already included in the educational curriculum both at schools and universities. Schools subsidised by the Board of Education are obliged to provide science-teaching.

---

①　Ananias and Sapphira：亚拿尼亚和撒非喇，二人为夫妇，因私扣变卖田产所得的钱欺骗圣灵而招致死亡。摘自《圣经·使徒行传》。撒非喇又译萨菲拉、瑟菲勒。

认，这种特别但又常见的无知确实暗示着，他们没有能力记住一个古老的传说。我们可能不大愿意承认这个事实：虽然大部分学理科的人有一些娱乐活动，甚至是艺术性的娱乐活动，但几乎毫无例外的是，他们没有积极融入这个世界。在我们这个世界里，文学、历史和艺术有立竿见影的价值，简简单单的解释就能说明我们多么需要这些学科。那么，上述两种缺陷哪一种更严重呢？对科学一无所知，会使一个人的心灵变得黑暗，而心灵孕育着一个民族的未来，因此，对科学的无知比对人类历史和人类奋斗的过程无知要危险得多。当然，我们也很难去质疑大众的意见：对万有引力一无所知，虽然荒谬，但可以原谅；对亚拿尼亚一无所知，绝对不可原谅。

这就是真正的困难之所在。这个国家的民众，确实更偏好非科学一类的学科，而鄙视科学一类的学科。不管他们的选择是对是错，都几乎不可逆转。改变公共观点的革命很少发生。自然，民主推崇众口之辞，但也会被众口之辞所动摇。自然，科学的目的和范畴，越来越超越一般民众理解的限度——甚至超越受教育者理解的限度，因而大众肯定会更看重自己熟悉的、灵活而多样的语言，而非沉闷、表达不清的自然哲学家的话。

在这些讨论中，人们往往忘记现在自然科学在中小学和大学的课程设置中都占有重要位置。由教育局提供经费的学校必须教授理科。公立学校也有教授物理和化学的设备，甚至是优良的设备。新建的大学设立了高水平而富有活力的理科学院。在历史较悠久的大学当中，剑桥大学以科研活动中心而著称。在几个理科领域，剑桥毫无疑问声名卓著。大学和学院可以自由使用自己的捐款促进理科的发展。理科研究不仅在物质

The public schools have equipment, in some cases a superb equipment, for teaching at least physics and chemistry. At the newer universities there are great and vigorous schools of science. Of the old universities Cambridge stands out as a chief centre of scientific activity. In several branches of science Cambridge is without question pre-eminent. The endowments both of the university and the colleges are freely used for the advancement of the sciences. Not only in these material ways are scientific studies in no sense neglected, but the position of the sciences is recognised and even envied by those who follow other kinds of learning. The scientific schools of Cambridge form perhaps the dominant force among the resident body of the university, and except by virtue of some great increase in the endowments, it would be impossible to extend further the scientific side of Cambridge and still maintain other forms of intellectual activity in such proportion as to preserve that healthy co-ordination which is the life of a great university.

At Oxford the case is no doubt very different. The measure in which the sciences are esteemed appears only too plainly in the small proportion of Fellowships filled by men of science. Progress has nevertheless begun. At the remarkable Conference called in May, 1916, to protest against the neglect of science it was noticeable that the speakers were, in overwhelming majority, Oxford men.

Among the educational institutions of England there is no general neglect to provide teaching of natural science and much of the language used in reference to the problem of reform is not really in accord with fact. Probably no boy able to afford a good secondary school, certainly none able to proceed to a university, is debarred from scientific teaching merely because it does not "form an integral part" of the curriculum. This alone suffices to prove that the real cause of the deplorable neglect of science is to be sought elsewhere. The fundamental difficulty is that which has been already indicated, that public taste and judgment deliberately prefers the type known as literary, or as it might with more propriety be designated, "vocal." In the schools there is no lack of science teaching, but the small percentage of boys whose minds develop early and whose general capacity for learning and aptitude for affairs mark them out as leaders, rarely have much instinct for science, and avoid such teaching, finding it irksome and unsatisfying. These it is, who going afterwards

方面没有被忽视，在精神上其地位也得到了承认，甚至被其他学科所嫉妒。剑桥的理科学院，可能是学校院系中的中坚力量，因此学校为其争取的捐款增长很快，但学校促进理科发展的措施也仅此而已，否则不可能同时保持其他知识活动的恰当比例，从而使学科间达到了平衡——而不同学科间的健康与均衡发展，正是一所大学的灵魂。

在牛津，情况则大不一样。理科的地位很一般，采取的措施很简单，获得奖学金的理科生比例很小。当然，现在情况也有所改善。在 1916 年 5 月召开的那场令人瞩目的会议上，抗议理科遭到忽视的人中，绝大多数是牛津人士。

在英格兰的教育机构中，自然科学的教育并没有被普遍忽视，只不过很多关于这个问题的改革方面的言谈其实和事实不符。有能力支付一所优良中学学费的学生，或者有能力进入大学深造的学生，都不会因为理科不是整个课程"密不可分"的一部分，而没有机会接受理科教育。这个事实本身就足以证明，这种令人可悲的对于科学的忽视必须从其他地方寻找原因。如上所述，最根本的困难在于大众的审美和判断自发地偏向文学之类的东西，也许因此这一类的东西更有利于自由地发表意见。在学校里，理科教育其实并不缺乏，但是那些少数心智发育较早，学习能力和事务管理能力出众的学生，很少天生就对理科感兴趣，反而觉得理科沉闷而枯燥，常常不愿意学习。他们在进入大学以后——当然绝大部分去了牛津，为自己营造了一种融洽的氛围，这种氛围偶尔会被一阵涟漪打破，那就是知识的革命。正是在知识的革命中，一种新的文明格局正在形成。观察到他们的力量取决于他们拥有的特殊天赋，这种天赋让他们在民主政府的领导

to the universities, in preponderating numbers to Oxford, make for themselves a congenial atmosphere, disturbed only by faint ripples of that vast intellectual renascence in which the new shape of civilisation is forming. With self-complacency unshaken, they assume in due course charge of Church and State, the Press, and in general the leadership of the country. As lawyers and journalists they do our talking for us, let who will do the thinking. Observe that their strength lies in the possession of a special gift, which under the conditions of democratic government has a prodigious opportunity. Uncomfortable as the reflection may be, it is not to be denied that the countries in which science has already attained the greatest influence and recognition in public affairs are Germany and Japan, where the opinions of the ignorant are not invited. But facts must be recognised, and our government is likely to remain in the hands of those who have the gift of speech. A general substitution of scientific men for the "vocal" could scarcely be achieved, even if the change were desirable. The utmost limit of success which the conditions admit is some inoculation of scientific interest and ideas upon the susceptible members of the classes already preferred. That a large proportion of those persons are in the biological sense resistant to all such influences must be expected. Granting however that a section perhaps even the majority, of our [Greek: beltistoi] may prove unamenable to the influences of science no one can doubt that under the present system of education a proportion of not unintelligent boys in practice have little option. From earliest youth classics are offered to them as almost the sole vehicle of education. They do sufficiently well in classics, as they probably would on any other curriculum, to justify themselves and their advisers in thinking that they have made a good beginning to which it is safer to stick. The system has a huge momentum, and so, holding to the "great wheel" ① that goes up the hill, they let it draw them after. In their protest against the monotony of the courses provided for young boys the reformers are right. The trouble is not that science is not taught in the schools, but that in schools of the highest type, with certain exceptions, the young boys are not offered it.

---

① great wheel: 此处可能是指希腊神话故事中西西弗斯所推动的那块巨石。西西弗斯触犯了诸神，诸神为了惩罚他，便要求他把一块巨石推上山顶，而由于那巨石太重了，每次未到山顶就又滚下山去，前功尽弃，于是他就不断重复、永无止境地做这件事——诸神认为做这种无效无望的劳动是最严厉的惩罚。西西弗斯的生命就在这样一种无效又无望的劳动当中慢慢耗尽。作者是想用此比喻以古典文学为主的教育体系。

下有着巨大的机会。他们扬扬得意，坚信在不久的未来，他们就会掌控教会和国家，掌控新闻媒体，然后掌控整个国家的领导权。既然律师和记者掌握了我们的发言权，更不用说那些掌握思想的人。虽然这种反思可能令人不快，但不可否认的是，在德国和日本这样的国家，科学在公共事务中的作用得到了普遍的承认，发挥了巨大的影响，那些愚昧的观点也就很难盛行了。相反，我们必须承认，我们的政府权力更倾向于保留在那些具有演说天赋的人手中。要想用具有科学头脑的人代替这些会说话的人，即使这样做是正确的，也几乎是不可能的。目前情况下，最好的办法可能就是让那些公众偏好的阶层中易于接受新鲜事物的人，多少培养一些科学的兴趣，接受一些科学的观点。可以想象，这个阶层中的大部分人对这种科学的影响从本能上有一种抗拒。考虑到我们中的一部分人，甚至是大部分人，没有义务接受科学的影响，因此，不可否认，在现行的教育体制下，那些聪颖的学生有一部分在实践中几乎没有其他选择。从最初的阶段开始，古典文学对他们来说就是教育的唯一载体。正如他们可能把其他学科学得很好一样，他们在这些科目上也做得很好，以此说服他们自己和他们的导师，他们已经取得了一个良好的开端，并可以顺利地继续下去。这个体系有巨大的动能，因此有能量把那个"巨大车轮"推到山顶，而他们就跟在后面。当改革者抱怨学生的课程太单调时，他们的确是对的，但问题不是学校里没有教授理科课程，而是即使在最优秀的学校，除个别情况外，学生也几乎没有机会学习理科课程。

现代生物学知识促使我们接受决定论的观点，不过我们对教育对个体命运影响相对较小的这种观点持怀

Realising the determinism which modern biological knowledge has compelled us to accept, we suspect that the power of education to modify the destinies of individuals is relatively small. Abrogating larger hopes we recognise education in its two scientific aspects, as a selective agency, but equally as a provision of opportunity. In view therefore of the congenital diversity of the individual types, that provision should be as diverse and manifold as possible, and the very first essential in an adequate scheme of education is that to the minds of the young something of everything should be offered, some part of all the kinds of intellectual sustenance in which the minds of men have grown and rejoiced. That should be the ideal. Nothing of varied stimulus or attraction that can be offered should be withheld. So only will the young mind discover its aptitudes and powers. This ideal education should bring all into contact with *beauty* as seen first in literature, ancient and modern, with the great models of art and the patterns of nobility of thought and of conduct; and no less should it show to all the *truth* of the natural world, the changeless systems of the universe, as revealed in astronomy or in chemistry, something too of the truth about life, what we animals really are, what our place and what our powers, a truth ungarbled whether by prudery or mysticism.

But presented with this ideal the schoolmaster will reply that something of everything means nothing *thorough*. I know the objection and what it commonly stands for. It is the cloak and pretext for that accursed pedantry and cant which turns every sort of teaching to a blight. Thoroughness is the excuse for giving boys grammar and accidence in the name of Greek: diagrams, formulae and numerical examples in the name of science. Stripped of disguise this love of thoroughness is nothing but an indolent resolve to make things easy for the teacher, and, worse still, for the examiner. Live teaching is hard work. It demands continual freshness and a mind alert. The dullest man can hear irregular verbs, and with the book he knows whether they are said right or wrong, but to take a text and show what the passage means to the world, to reconstruct the scene and the conditions in which it was written, to show the origins and the fruits of ideas or of discoveries, demand qualities of a very different order. The plea for thoroughness may no doubt be offered in perfect sincerity. There are plenty of men, especially among those who desire the office of a pedagogue, whose

疑态度。抛开对教育更大的期望，我们希望从两个方面来科学地认识教育：一是教育具有选择性；二是教育能够提供机会。因此，考虑到每个个体与生俱来的多样性，教育应当尽量多样化、多形式化。同时，一个完善的教育计划最核心的精神应该是：对于年轻的心灵，每种东西都应该提供一点，人类的心灵成长所需要和所喜欢的每一种知识营养都应该提供一点。这当然很理想。但是，我们至少不应该去阻止那些多样化的刺激和吸引。只有这样，年轻人才能发掘他们真正的才能。理想的教育应当把一切和美联系起来，就像在文学中首先感受到的一样——无论是古代文学还是现代文学；把一切和伟大的艺术形式以及高尚的思想行为联系起来。同样，理想的教育还应该不遗余力地展现自然界的真实，天文学和化学所显示的宇宙的永恒，生命的真谛，包括我们人类的动物的本质，我们地球的本质，我们力量的源泉。这些真谛是神秘主义和伪道学都无法改变的。

然而，随之而来的是，有些校长可能会说每样东西都学一点，意味着每样都难以*精通*。我理解这种反对和这种反对通常所代表的意思。这不过是一个借口，一个把每一种教学都变得枯燥乏味的冠冕堂皇的借口。"精通"是以希腊语的名义教授语法和词形变化的借口，是以科学的名义要求学生学习图表、公式、数值例子的借口。撕开伪装，这种对"精通"的热爱只不过是一种把一切教学简单化的懒惰行为，而且考试也因此可以更好处理。教学要做到生动是非常困难的，这需要保持教学内容新颖，教师思维敏捷。沉闷乏味的教师能辨认不规则动词；拿着书，他知道学生说的是对的还是错的。但是，如果让他拿一篇课文，解释这篇课文有什么社会意义，再现这篇文章的写作背景

field of vision is constricted to a slit. If they were painters their work would be in the slang of the day, "tight." One small group of facts they see hard and sharp, without atmosphere or value. Their own knowledge having no capacity for extension, no width or relationship to the world at large, they cannot imagine that breadth in itself may be a merit. Adepts in a petty erudition without vital antecedents or consequences, they would willingly see the world shrivel to the dimensions of their own landscape.

Anticipating here the applause of the reforming party, to avoid misapprehension let it be expressly observed that pedantry of this sort is in no sense the special prerogative of teachers of classics. We meet it everywhere. Among teachers of science the type abounds, and from the papers set in any Natural Sciences Tripos, not to speak of scholarship examinations of every kind, it would be possible to extract question after question that ought never to have been set, referring to things that need never have been taught, and knowledge that no one but a pedant would dream of carrying in his head for a week.

The splendid purpose which science serves is the inculcation of principle and balance, not facts. There is something horrible and terrifying in the doctrine so often preached, reiterated of course by speaker after speaker at the "Neglect of Science" meeting, that science is to be preferred because of its utility. If the choice were really between dead classics and dead science, or if science is to be vivified by an infusion of commercial, utilitarian spirit, then a thousand times rather let us keep to the classics as the staple of education. They at least have no "use." At least they hold the keys to the glorious places, to the fulness of literature and to the thoughtful speech of all kindred nations, nor are they demeaned with sordid, shop-keeper utility. This was plainly in the mind of the Poet Laureate, who speaking at the meeting I have referred to, said well that "a merely utilitarian science can never win the spiritual respect of mankind." The main objection that the humanists make to the introduction of natural science as a necessary subject of education, is, he declared, that science is not spiritual, that it does not work in the sphere of ideas. He went on very properly to show how perverse is such a representation of science, but, alas, in further recommendation of science as a safe subject of instruction he added that the antagonism of science to religion is ended, and that the contest had been a

和情景、文章思想和内容的起源与意义，他就无能为力了，这些需要很多完全不同的素质。当然，也有些人是出于完全诚实的态度来提出"精通"的想法。很多人，尤其那些希望致力于小学教育的人，他们的视野非常狭隘，如果他们是画家，他们的作品只能用俚语"紧"来形容。他们把一小部分事实看得既严重又死板，从不考虑氛围和价值。他们自身的知识没有广度，没有宽度，没有从宏观上和世界联系起来，所以他们也认识不到广度本身就是一个优点。在狭隘的领域，他们宁愿把世界缩小到他们认识的范围内，既不考虑前因，也不考虑后果。

说到这儿，改革派可能会大为赞同。为了避免误解，有必要指出，这种狭隘而又迂腐的倾向并非只是古典文学教师才有的缺陷，我们到处都可能遇到。理科教师中这种类型也比比皆是，在每种自然科学荣誉学位考试中，在每一类奖学金考试中，所考查的一个个题目都是完全不应该出现的，考查的知识也是完全没有必要教授的，可能只有书呆子老师才会臆想这些知识是有用的，但这种臆想最多也就持续一周。

科学的宏伟目标是向大众灌输原理和"平衡"的思想，而非事实。在那些"忽视科学"的会议上，在一个又一个的发言人反复强调和推行的教条中，有一些令人恐怖的东西，那就是我们更偏爱科学是因为科学是"实用的"。如果要在僵化的古典文学和僵化的理科之间做选择，如果科学被商业和功利主义粉饰起来，那么即使选择一千次，我们也会坚持把古典文学作为教育的基础。至少它们没有"用处"。至少它们是通往那些光辉地方的关键，是通往丰富的文学作品的关键，是通往所有民族的有思想的演说的关键，而非肮脏的店员式的实用。这也是桂冠诗人的想法。在我参加的

passing phase. Reading this we may wonder whether we are in fairness entitled to Dr Bridges's approval. "Tastes sweet the water with such specks of earth?" [①] Since he spoke of the "unscientific attitude" of Professor Huxley as a thing of the past, candour obliges us to insist emphatically that the struggle continues and must perpetually be renewed. Huxley was opposing the teaching of science to that of revelation. In these days the ground has shifted, and supernatural teachings make preferably their defence by an appeal to intuition and other obscure phenomena which can be trusted to defy investigation. Against all such apocryphal glosses of evidential truth science protests with equal vehemence, and were Huxley [②] here he would treat Bergson and his allies with the same scorn and contumely that he meted out to the Bishop of Oxford on the notorious occasion to which Dr Bridges made reference. As well might we decorate our writings with Plantin title-pages, showing the author embraced by angels and inspiring muses, as recommend ourselves in these disguises.

Agnosticism is the very life and mainspring of science. Not merely as to the supernatural but as to the natural world must science believe nothing save under compulsion. Little of value has a man got from science who has not learned to be slow of faith. Those early lessons in the study of the natural world will be the best which most frankly declare our ignorance, exciting the mind to attack the unknown by showing how soon the frontier of knowledge is reached. "We don't know" should be

---

① "Tastes sweet the water with such specks of earth?"：这句话源自 Robert Browning（罗伯特·勃朗宁）的诗歌 *Pictor Ignotus* 最后一句。此处的意思是再完美的东西也有瑕疵。罗伯特·勃朗宁（1812~1889），维多利亚时期代表诗人之一，与丁尼生齐名。主要作品有《戏剧抒情诗》《剧中人物》《指环与书》等。他以精细入微的心理探索而独步诗坛，对 20 世纪英美诗歌产生了重要影响。其妻勃朗宁夫人也是著名诗人。

② Huxley：此处应指 Thomas Henry Huxley（汤玛斯·亨利·赫胥黎）（1825~1895），英国生物学家，因捍卫查尔斯·达尔文的进化论而被称为"达尔文的斗牛犬"（Darwin's Bulldog）。他为了对抗理查·欧文的理论而提出的科学论证显示出人类和大猩猩的脑部解剖具有很大的相似性。有趣的是赫胥黎并不完全接受达尔文的许多看法（例如渐进主义），而且，相对于捍卫物竞天择理论，他对提倡唯物主义科学精神更感兴趣。作为科普工作的倡导者，他提出了概念"不可知论"来形容他对宗教信仰的态度。他还因提出了生源论（biogenesis，认为一切细胞皆起源于其他细胞）以及无生源论（abiogenesis，认为生命来自无生命物质）的概念而广为人知。赫胥黎家族在英国学术界十分著名，包括他的孙子奥尔德斯·赫胥黎（作家）、朱利安·赫胥黎爵士（联合国教科文组织首任主席，创立世界自然基金会）、安德鲁·赫胥黎爵士（生理学家，诺贝尔奖得主）。

一个会议中，他说得很好：一种仅仅实用的科学绝不会赢得人类的尊重；人文主义者反对科学作为教育的一个必要学科的主要理由是，科学是非精神的，科学不是在思想领域运作的；事实正好相反，科学是教育中一门保险的学科，科学和宗教的对抗已经结束，它们之间的竞争已经成为过去。读到这儿，我们可能想知道，我们是否能同意布里奇博士的提议"带着灰尘品尝水的甜美"？因为他说到赫胥黎教授的"不科学的态度"已经是过去的事，我们不得不坦率地强调斗争还在继续，而且会不断更新。赫胥黎反对教授科学是因为《圣经》的启示。但这些天，反对的基础已经动摇，超自然的教学通过对本能的坚持和其他一些难以调查清楚的晦暗现象来捍卫自己，科学也同样激烈地反对这些虚伪、偶然的真实。如果赫胥黎在这儿，他会以同样的蔑视对待博格什和他们的同伙，他会在布里奇博士提出意见的场合批判牛津主教。其可能性之大，正如我们会用标题来装饰我们的作品，以示我们被天使和缪斯女神所眷顾。

不可知论是科学的起源和主流。不仅对超自然现象，而且对自然界，科学都绝不应该迷信，当然冲动之下，可能会有例外。如果一个人没有学会逐步接受事物，那他从科学中几乎不会有什么收获。在研究自然界的启蒙课程中，那些坦率地承认我们无知的课程，那些展示我们是如何到达知识的前沿，从而激起心灵去探索未知领域的课程，才是最好的课程。"我们不知道"这句话应该常常挂在老师的嘴边，接下来的一句话应该是"我们总会搞清楚"。不仅仅对研究者，对学生也一样，他们最感兴趣的领域是那些知识正在不断更新的领域。学生应该立刻了解这些东西，而我们当前的研究手段对这些科学领域的细节仅是泛泛表述，

ever in the mouth of the teacher, followed sometimes by "we may find out yet." Not merely to the investigator but to the pupil the interest of science is strongest in the growing edges of knowledge. The student should be transported thither with the briefest possible delay. Details of those parts of science which by present means of investigation are worked out and reduced to general expressions are dull and lifeless. Many and many a boy has been repelled, gathering from what he hears in class that science is a catalogue of names and facts interminable.

In childhood he may have felt curiosity about nature and the common impulse to watch and collect, but when he begins scientific lessons he discovers too often that they relate not even to the kind of fact which nature is for him, or to the subjects of his early curiosity and wonder, but to things that have no obvious interest at all, measurements of mechanical forces, reaction-formulae, and similar materials.

All these, it is true, man has gradually accumulated with infinite labour; upon them, and of such materials has the great fabric of science been reared: but to insist that the approaches to science shall be open only to those who will surmount these gratuitous obstacles is mere perversity. Men's minds do not work in that way. How many would discover the grandeur of a Gothic building if they were prevented from seeing one until they could work out stresses and strains, date mouldings, and even perhaps cut templates? Most of us, to be sure, enjoy the cathedrals more when we acquire some such knowledge, and those who are to be architects must acquire it, but we can scarcely be astonished if beginners turn away in disgust from science presented on those terms.

It is from considerations of this kind that I am led to believe that for most boys the easiest and most attractive introduction to science is from the biological side. Admittedly chemistry is the more fundamental study, and some rudimentary chemical notions must be imparted very early, but if the framework subject-matter be animals and plants, very sensible progress in realising what science means and aims at doing will have been made before the things of daily life are left behind. These first formal lessons in science should continue and extend the boy's own attempts to find out how the world is made.

枯燥而无味。许许多多的学生，从课堂上积累的知识中，不得不得出一个结论——科学只是一个冗长的名称和事实列表。

在童年时期，一个人可能会对自然感到好奇，一般会有观察和收集的冲动，但是开始学习科学课程的时候，他常常会发现这些课程和他所了解的自然界事实无关，或者和他童年时期感到好奇的东西无关，而是和他完全没有明显兴趣的东西相关，比如机械力的测量、化学反应公式以及类似的东西。

的确，所有的这些知识，人类是通过无数艰苦的努力逐渐积累起来的，正是在这些原理和材料之上，科学才慢慢发展起来。但是如果坚持只有已经掌握了这些知识、已经克服了这些巨大障碍的人，才能去学习和研究科学的话，结果只会适得其反，人类的大脑不是以这样的方式思考的。如果一个人只有在计算出压力和拉力、日期模型，甚至能剪切模板之后，才能看到具体的建筑，那么我们当中有多少人能够欣赏一座哥特式建筑的宏伟呢？当然，我们中的大多数，如果学习了上述知识，能更好地欣赏哥特式的教堂，那些想成为建筑师的人，就必须学习这些知识。但是，如果一个初学者面对这些术语会厌恶科学，拒绝学习科学，我们也绝不会感到惊讶。

考虑到这些，我相信，从生物学的角度出发，对大多数学生而言，科学入门课程应该越简单、越吸引人越好。大家都认为化学是最基础的课程，一些基础的化学概念应该尽早教授，但是如果基本大纲的主要内容是动物和植物，那么应该先让学生认识到科学意味着什么，科学的目的是什么，然后再学习日常生活的知识。这种正式的科学课程应该鼓励学生自己尝试发现这个世界。

I shall be charged with running counter both to common sense and to authority in expressing parenthetically the further conviction that, in biology at least, laboratory work is now largely overdone. Whether this is so at schools I cannot tell, but at the universities whole mornings and afternoons spent in making elaborate preparations, drawings and series of sections, are frequently wasted. These courses were devised with the highest motives. Students were to "find out everything for themselves." Generally they are doing nothing of the kind. It may have been so once, but with text-books perfected and teaching stereotyped, the more industrious are slavishly verifying what has been verified repeatedly, or at best acquiring manipulative skill. The rest are doing nothing whatever. They would be better employed taking a walk, devilling for some investigator, browsing in museums or libraries, or even arguing with each other. Certainly a few lessons in the use of indexes and books of reference would be far more valuable. Students of every grade must of course do some laboratory work, and all should see as much material as possible. My protest is solely against those long, torpid hours compulsorily given to labour which will lead to nothing of novelty, and serves only to teach what can be got readily in other ways. There are a few whose souls crave such employment. By all means let them follow it.

But whatever is good for maturer students, biology for schoolboys should be of a less academic cast.

The natural history of animals and plants has the obvious merit that it prolongs the inborn curiosity of youth, that its subject-matter is universally at hand, accessible in holidays and in the absence of teachers or laboratories, and best of all that through biological study the significance of science appears immediately, disclosing the true story of man's relation to the world. From natural history the transition to the other sciences, especially to chemistry and physics, is easy and again natural. In the study of life many of the fundamental conceptions of those sciences are met with on the threshold, and boys whose aptitudes are rather of the physical order will at once feel the impulse to follow nature from that aspect. Biology is the more inclusive study. A man may be a good chemist and miss the broad meaning of science altogether, being sometimes indeed more devoid of such comprehension than many a philosopher fresh

　　无论从常识的角度，还是从权威的观点来看，都可以进一步相信，至少在生物学学科上，实验做得太多了。我不敢说在中小学也是如此，但在大学，整个上午和下午都常常浪费在那些复杂的实验准备、绘图和一系列的实验上。这些课程是以最高的要求来设计的，学生要"自己发现一切"。通常的结果是，他们所做的工作完全达不到这个目的。可能在以前这样做是有效的，但随着教科书不断改进，教学越来越模式化，越用功的学生越会发现他们其实只不过在毫无创见地证明已经被反复证明过的东西，或者最多就是学习一些操作技巧。而其他的学生，则一无所获。所花的这些时间，学生完全可以用来散散步，给某些研究员做做助手，到博物馆或图书馆看看，甚至学生之间进行讨论。当然，少数如何使用参考书和索引的课程要有价值得多。每一个年级的学生，都应该做一些实验，所有学生都应该认识不同的材料，越多越好。我仅仅反对把大量的时间花在毫无新意的工作上，其实用其他方法也完全可以教会学生这些东西。有一些学生非常渴望这样做，而且也千方百计这样做了。

　　对于大学生而言，有益的课程可能很多，但对中小学生而言，生物学一定不要过于学术化。

　　动植物的自然史对年轻人而言，有明显的好处，因为可以延续他们天生的好奇心，相关的事物唾手可得；在假期，当老师不在场、实验室不能用时也可以学习。通过学习生物课程最大的好处是，科学的意义可以立刻显现，即揭示出人和这个世界的真正关系。从自然界的历史出发，转而学习其他科学方面的学科，尤其是化学和物理，既自然又简单。在研究生命的本质的时候，很多其他学科的基本概念一入门就会遇到，那些天生热爱物理规则的学生，马上会有一种从这个方面研究自然的冲动。生物是一门综合性的学科，有助于拓宽一个人的

from Classical Greats.

In appealing for a progress from the general to the particular I am not blind to the dangers. Biology for the young readily degenerates into a mawkish "nature-study," or all-for-the-best claptrap about adaptation, but a sure remedy is the strong tonic of agnosticism, teaching one of the best lessons science has to offer, the resolute rejection of authority.

Some take comfort in the hope that all subjects may be taught as branches of science, but the fact that must permanently postpone arrival at this educational Utopia is that a great proportion of teachers are not and can never be made scientific. Nothing proceeding from such persons will by the working of any schedule, regulation, or even Order of the Board be ever made to bear any colourable resemblance to science. Moreover as has already been indicated, there are plenty of pupils also who will flourish and probably reach their highest development taught by unscientific men, pupils whose minds would be sterilised or starved by that very nourishment which to our thinking is the more generous. Were we a homogeneous population one diet for all might be justifiable, but as things are, we should offer the greatest possible variety.

From Rousseau onwards educationists, deriving their views, I suppose, from some metaphysical or theological conception of human equality, speak continually of the "mind of the child" as if the young of our species conformed to a single type. If the general spread of biological knowledge serves merely to expose that foolish assumption there would be progress to record. Dr Blakeslee, a well-known American biologist, lately gave a good illustration of this. In a paper on education he showed photographs of two varieties of maize. The ripe fruits of both are colourless if their sheaths be unbroken. The one, if exposed to the light before ripening, by rupture of its sheath, turns red. The second, otherwise indistinguishable, acquires no red colour though uncovered to the full sun. If these maizes were two boys, not improbably the one would be caned for failing to respond to treatment so efficacious in the case of the other. When we hear that such a man has developed too exclusively one side of his nature, with what propriety do we assume that he had any other side to develop? Or when we say that such-and-such a course of study tends to make boys too

视野。一个人可能成为一名优秀的化学家，与此同时完全忽视科学的宽泛意义，而自己还完全没有意识到这个问题，这简直比很多哲学家居然不知道那些古代伟人还要糟糕。

在呼吁科学教学应该取得从普遍到具体的进步的时候，我也注意到某些危险。为年轻人开设的生物课很容易退化为枯燥的"自然研究"或者哗众取宠的适应论，好在有一个解决问题的良方，就是坚持不可知论，科学所教给学生最好的道理就是：绝不盲从权威。

有些人希望所有的学科都作为科学的分支来教授，并对此感到欣慰。但事实上，这个乌托邦式的教育理想永远也不能实现，因为很大一部分教师现在和将来都无法变得具有科学性。无论推行什么计划、规定，甚至教育部门的命令，这类人都很难进步，很难变得哪怕具有一点点类似科学的特性。而且，正如上文所述，很多学生由不具有科学性的老师教导，也同样茁壮成长，甚至发展到个人可能达到的最高境界。我们在内心可能更愿意认为，这样有限的滋养也许会导致学生心灵的枯萎。假如人类是同一种人，那么对所有人而言，一个食谱就足够，但事实正好相反，那我们就应该尽可能提供多样化的选择。

总结自卢梭以来的教育家的观点，从形而上学的观点到神学方面有关人类平等的概念，都不断提及"孩子的心灵"，好像就人类这个物种而言，年轻人的心灵只有一种。如果生物学知识的推广仅仅是为了揭示这个愚蠢的假设，倒是应该把这个进步记录下来。美国著名生物学家布莱克斯利博士最近就此提供一个很好的例子。在一篇论及教育的文章中，他展示了两种不同的玉米的照片。如果两种玉米的外皮都没有裂开，它们的果实最后都没有颜色。其中一种，如果外皮裂开，在成熟前受到

exclusively literary, or scientific, or what not, do we not really mean that it provides too exclusively for those whose aptitudes are of these respective kinds? Living in the midst of a mongrel population we note the divers powers of our fellows and we thoughtlessly imagine that if something different had happened to us, we can't say what, we should have been able to rival them. A little honest examination of our powers shows how vain are such suppositions. The right course is to make some provision for all sorts, since unscientific teaching and unscientific persons will remain with us always.

Teaching of this universal and undifferentiated sort, provided for all in common, should be continued up to the age at which pupils begin to show their tastes and aptitudes, in general about 16, after which stage such latitude of choice should be given as the resources of the school can provide.

Of what should the undifferentiated teaching consist? Coming from a cultivated home a boy of 10 may be expected to have learned the rudiments of Latin, and at least one modern language, preferably French, *colloquially*, arithmetic, outlines of geography, tales from Plutarch [①] and from other histories. Going to a preparatory school he will read easy Latin texts *with translations* and notes; French books, geography including the elements of astronomy, beginning also algebra and geometry. At 12 dropping French except perhaps a reading once a week, he will begin Greek, by means of easy passages again with the translations beside him, continuing the rest as before. Transferred at 14-1/2 to a public school he will go on with Latin, starting Latin prose, Greek texts, again read fast with translations. He will now have his first formal introduction to science in the guise of biology, leading up to lessons and demonstrations in chemistry and physics. At about 16-1/2 he may drop classics *or mathematics* according as his tastes have declared themselves, adding modern languages instead, continuing science in all cases, greater or less in amount according

---

① Plutarch：普鲁塔克（46~120），是一位用希腊文写作的罗马传记文学家、散文家以及柏拉图学派的知识分子，著作极其丰硕，传世之作为《希腊罗马名人传》（*Plutarch's Lives*）和《掌故清谈录》（*Moralia*），尤以前者更为脍炙人口，对后世影响最大。莎士比亚的三部戏剧，很多情节是根据其传说作品的内容，英国一位传记家鲍威尔更是将普鲁塔克尊为"传记之王"。

光线的照射，果实会变成红色。另外一种，其他情况完全一样，只是外皮没有裂开，虽然也接受了足够的阳光，果实却没有变红。如果这两种玉米是两个学生，后者肯定会被打手板，因为他没有在另外一种条件下做出同样有效的反应。当我们听说某个人把他本性中一面发展到了极致，我们有什么理由假设，他其实可能在其他方面也发展得很好？或者说，当我们认为这一门或那一门课程会让学生仅仅发展文学才能或者理科才能，可能抑制了学生发展其他才能，难道我们真正的意思不是"这门课其实是为那些在文学或者理科方面有天赋的学生提供的"吗？生活在鱼龙混杂的人群中，我们注意到人们的多样性，并轻率地设想，即使有什么不同发生了，我们也不会说什么，因为我们完全可以应付这样的情况。如果诚实地审视一下我们的力量，就会发现这种假设毫无作用。正确的做法是为各种不同的人群提供一些不同的选择，因为不科学的教学和不科学的人将永远存在。

这种对所有人一视同仁的教学，只能持续到学生开始有了自己的审美和倾向为止——一般来说到16岁左右的时候。从这以后，学校就应该根据自己的资源，尽量提供多样化的选择。

那么这种无差别的教学应该包含什么内容？一个从书香门第出来的10岁的学生，应该已经学习了拉丁文的基础知识、至少一门现代通俗语言（当然最好是法语），以及算术、地理基本知识、普鲁塔克故事或者其他历史故事。这样，上了预备学校，他们就可以轻松地读一些*带有翻译*和注释的拉丁课文，开始学习代数和几何。在12岁的时候，除了每周读点读物外，法语可以放下了，应该开始学习希腊语，可以先读点配有翻译的简单文章，同时以前所学的科目也要继续。14岁半上中学的时候，应该继续学习拉丁语，开始阅读配有翻译的拉丁语散文

to his proclivities.

Boys with special mathematical ability will of course need special treatment. Moreover provision of German for all has avowedly not been made. For all it is desirable and for many indispensable. But as the number who read it for pleasure, never very large, seems likely to diminish, German may perhaps be reserved as a tool, the use of which must be acquired when necessary.

Such a scheme, I submit, makes no impossible demand on the time-table, allowing indeed many spare hours for accessory subjects such as readings in English or history. Note the main features of this programme. The time for things worth learning is found by dropping *grammar* as a subject of special study. There are to be no lessons in grammar or accidence as such, nor of course any verse compositions except for older boys specialising in classics. *Mathematics* also is treated as a subject which need not be carried beyond the rudiments unless mathematical or physical ability is shown. For other boys it leads literally nowhere, being a road impassable.

All the languages are to be taught as we learn them in later life, when the desire or necessity arises, by means of easy passages with the translation at our side. Our present practice not only fails to teach languages but it succeeds in teaching how *not* to learn a language. Who thinks of beginning Russian by studying the "aspects" of the verbs, or by committing to memory the 28 paradigms which German grammarians have devised on the analogy of Latin declensions? Auxiliary verbs are the pedagogue's delight, but who begins Spanish by trying to discriminate between *tener* and *haber*, or *ser* and *estar*, or who learns tables of exceptions to improve his French? These things come by use or not at all.

If languages are treated not as lessons but as vehicles of speech, and if the authors are read so that we may find out what they say and how they say it, and at such a pace that we follow the train of thought or the story, all who have any sense of language at all can attend and with pleasure too. What chance has a boy of enjoying an author when he knows him only as a task to be droned through, thirty lines at a time? Small blame to the pupil who never discovers that the great authors were men of like passions with ourselves, that the Homeric songs were made to be shouted

和希腊语课文，速度应该加快。可以开始以生物学为借口，接受正规的科学启蒙，学习化学和物理的课程和实验。到 16 岁半的时候，他可以根据自己的兴趣，放下古典文学或者数学，增加现代语言。无论如何都理应继续理科课程，只是学习多少可以视自己的爱好而定。

在数学方面有天赋的学生当然要特殊对待。有关方面没有公开要求所有人学习德语，但学习这门语言对大家来说都有好处，对有些人来说甚至是必不可少的。少数人学习德语纯粹出于个人兴趣，学的人也越来越少，所以德语可以用来作为一种工具，有必要的时候，一定要学会使用这门语言。

这样一个计划，我认为在时间上是完全可行的，事实上还留有很多空余时间学习其他辅助课程，比如英语阅读和历史阅读。请注意，这个计划的主要特点是没有把*语法*列为一个专门学习的科目，这就为其他值得学习的东西腾出了时间。除了对那些年龄大一些的古典文学专业的学生，其他学生既没有语法、词法方面的课程，也没有任何诗歌写作课程；同样，数学也仅仅作为一门基础课程，并没有教授太复杂的东西，当然对那些有数学或物理天赋的学生会有所不同。因为对一般学生而言，很难走上数学专业的道路。

如果学生有意学习或者有必要的话，学校会教授所有的语言，其具体方法是提供带翻译的简单文章，就像我们在生活中学习语言一样。而我们现在的做法，不但没有好好教授语言，反而在阻挠外语学习上特别成功。有谁认为初学俄语应该学习动词的变位，或者初学德语应该记住语法学家总结的德语和拉丁语中类似的 28 种变位？助动词只有老师才喜欢，有谁在学习西班牙语的时候是从区分 tener 和 haber、ser 和 estar 开始的，又有谁是背特殊语法表来提高法语水平的？这些东西在实践中很

at feasts to heroes full of drink and glory, that Herodotus [①] is telling of wonders that his friends, and we too, want to hear, that in the tragedies we hear the voice of Sophocles [②] dictating, choked with emotion and tears; that even Roman historians wrote because they had something to tell, and Caesar, dull proser that he is, composed the *Commentaries* not to provide us with style or grammatical curiosities, but as a record of extraordinary events. To get into touch with any author he must be read at a good pace, and by reading of that kind there is plenty of time for a boy before he reaches 17 to make acquaintance with much of the best literature both of Greek and Latin.

Education must be brought up to date; but if in accomplishing that, we lose Greek, it will have been sacrificed to obstinate formalism and pedagogic tradition. The defence of classics as a basis of education is generally misrepresented by opponents. The unique value of the classics is not in any begetting of literary style. We are thinking of readers not of writers. Much of the best literature is the work of unlettered men, as they never tire of telling us, but it is for the enjoyment and understanding of books and of the world that continuity with the past should be maintained. John Bunyan wrote sterling prose, knowing no language but his own. But how much could he read? What judgments could he form? We want also to keep classics and especially Greek as the bountiful source of material and of colour, decoration for the jejune lives of common men. If classics cease to be generally taught and become the appanage of a few scholars, the gulf between the literary and the scientific will be made still wider. Milton will need more explanatory notes than O. Henry. Who will trouble about us scientific students then? We shall be marked off from the beginning, and in the world

---

① Herodotus: 希罗多德，公元前 5 世纪（约公元前 484~ 前 425 年）的古希腊作家，他把旅行中的所闻所见，以及第一波斯帝国的历史记录下来，著成《历史》一书，成为西方文学史上第一部完整流传下来的散文作品。

② Sophocles: 索福克勒斯（公元前 496~ 前 406 年），古希腊三大悲剧家之一。出身于兵器制造厂厂主家庭，生活于雅典极盛时期，是雅典民主派领袖伯里克利的朋友，曾任雅典税务委员会主席，被选为雅典十将军之一。但他在艺术上的成就远远胜过政治上的业绩。他从事戏剧创作 60 多年，写了 120 多部剧本，获奖 24 次，但是完整流传的剧本只有 7 部悲剧，其中最著名的是《俄狄浦斯王》。

少用到，或者根本不会用到。

如果语言不是被当作一门课程，而是被当作发言的工具；如果我们阅读某个作者是为了搞清楚他想表达的内容，他是用什么方式表达的，并在这种情况下跟随作者的思想或故事的线索，那么，任何人只要有一丁点语感，就能学会语言，并从中获得快乐。相反如果一个学生，把了解一个作家当成一项任务，老师也只是反复单调地解释一小段作品，比如30行字，学生怎么可能会喜欢这个作家？我们几乎不能责怪学生，因为他们没有发现那些伟大的作家是和我们一样满怀激情的人。荷马的史诗写出来，是为了在宴会上大声朗读给那些满身荣耀的醉醺醺的英雄；希罗多德写出传奇故事，只不过是因为他的朋友想听——当然我们也想；在悲剧中，我们听到了索福克勒斯的声音，虽然因为激动而满眶含泪、哽咽难言；即使是古罗马的历史学家，他们写作也是因为想倾诉某些东西；恺撒大帝，虽说是一个蹩脚的散文家，却写出了《高卢战记》，这当然不是出于语法或者风格上的好奇心，而是想记录一些特别的事件。要了解任何一位作家，学生必须有一个细致的计划和安排，这样的话，在他17岁之前，有大量的时间了解最优秀的希腊和拉丁文学作品。

教育当然必须与时俱进，但是如果为了做到这一点，我们丢掉了古希腊文化，那教育可能会被完全牺牲掉，只剩下形式主义和教条主义。我们必须确保古典作品作为教育基础的地位，这一点常常被反对者误解。古典作品的价值不仅仅在于其文学风格。我们是从读者而非作者的角度考虑问题的。很多最好的文学作品反而是不识字的人写出来的，他们反复向我们阐述一个意思：为了更好地欣赏和理解书本、更好地欣赏和理解世界，一定要记住过去。约翰·班扬仅仅懂本国语言，却写出了纯正

of laboratories Hector [①] , Antigone [②] and Pericles [③] will soon share the fate of poor Ananias and Sapphira.

I come now to the gravest part of the whole question. We plead for the preservation of literature, especially classical literature, as the staple of education in the name of beauty and understanding: but no less do we demand science in the name of truth and advancement. Given that our demand succeeds, what consequences may we expect? Nothing immediate, as I fear. In opening the discussion it was argued that even if scientific knowledge be widely diffused, any great change in the composition of the ruling classes is scarcely attainable under present conditions of social organisation. Even if science stand equal with classics in examinations for the services the general tenor of the public mind will in all likelihood be undisturbed. Yet it is for such a revolution that science really calls, and come it will in any community dominated by natural knowledge. Science saves us from blunders about glycerine, shows how to economise fuel and to make artificial nitrates, but these, though they decide national destinies, are merely the sheaf of the wave-offering: the harvest is behind. For natural knowledge is destined to give man not only a direct control of the material world but new interpretations of higher problems. Though we in England make a stand upon the ancient way, peoples elsewhere will move on. Those who have grasped the meaning of science, especially biological science, are feeling after new rules of conduct. The old criteria based on ignorance

① Hector：赫克托尔，普里阿摩斯（Priamus）的儿子，特洛伊（Troy）王子，帕里斯（Paris）的哥哥。他是特洛伊第一勇士，被称为"特洛伊的城墙"，最后和阿喀琉斯（Achilles）决斗，死在对方手里。

② Antigone：安提戈涅，古希腊悲剧作家索福克勒斯作品《安提戈涅》中的主人公。《安提戈涅》被公认为戏剧史上最伟大的作品之一。该剧在剧情上是忒拜三部曲中的最后一部，但完成最早。剧中描写了俄狄浦斯的女儿安提戈涅不顾国王克瑞翁的禁令，将自己的兄长、反叛城邦的波吕尼刻斯安葬，因而被处死，一意孤行的国王也遭妻离子散的命运。剧中人物性格饱满，剧情发展丝丝相扣。安提戈涅更是被塑造成维护神权/自然法而不向世俗权势低头的伟大女英雄形象，激发了后世的许多思想家如黑格尔、克尔凯郭尔、德里达等的哲思。

③ Pericles：伯里克利（约公元前495~前429年），古希腊奴隶主民主政治的杰出代表，古代世界最著名的政治家之一。

的散文诗。但他读了多少书呢？他又有什么样的判断呢？我们想保留古典作品，尤其是古希腊作品，因为这是不同物质条件、不同肤色的人丰富的文化源泉，是普通人枯燥生活的点缀。如果不再教授古典作品，仅有少数学者才能接触它们，那么文学和科学之间的鸿沟只会越来越宽。解释弥尔顿本来就要比解释欧·亨利需要更多的注释。这样的话，谁还会为理科学生考虑呢？他们可能从一开始就被排除在文学世界之外了，而在实验室的世界里，赫克托尔、安提戈涅和伯里克利很快就会沦为和可怜的亚拿尼亚和撒非喇一样的命运，被大家忘在脑后。

现在我来谈谈整个问题中最重要的部分。从美和理解的角度出发，我们呼吁保留文学，尤其是把古典文学作为教育的基础；同样，从真理和进步的角度来看，我们需要理科。如果我们的呼吁成功了，会有什么样的结果呢？没有立竿见影的效果，这也正是我所害怕的。在展开这场讨论的时候，就有人提出，即使广泛地传播科学知识，在现有的社会结构下，统治阶层的组成也不会发生太大的变化。即使理科和古典文学在考试中占据了同样的位置，公众心理也不会发生太大的改变。但科学真正要唤起的正是一场心灵的革命，真正要带来的是具有自然知识的群众。科学知识能把我们从"甘油"口误的危险中拯救出来，能指导我们节约能源、制造人工硝酸，等等，但所有这些，虽然会决定国家的命运，但其实仅仅是改革浪潮的表面影响，真正的收获还在后面。因为自然知识注定要赋予人类的，不仅仅是对物质世界的掌控，还有对更高层次问题的新阐释。虽然我们英格兰人仍然把重点放在传统的方式与方法上，但世界上其他地方的人总在前进。那些已经了解了科学的意义尤其是生物科学的意义的民族，正在尝试新的行为模式。基于愚昧无知的旧的标准已经毫无价值。民族或者国家的

have little worth. "Rights," whether of persons or of nations, may be abstractions well-founded in law or philosophy, but the modern world sooner or later will annul them.

The general ignorance of science has lasted so long that we have virtually two codes of right and duty, that founded on natural truth and that emanating from tradition, which almost alone finds public expression in this country. Whether we look at the cruelty which passes for justice in our criminal courts, at the prolongation of suffering which custom demands as a part of medical ethics, at this very question of education, or indeed at any problem of social life, we see ahead and know that science proclaims wiser and gentler creeds. When in the wider sphere of national policy we read the declared ideals of statesmen, we turn away with a shrug. They bid us exalt national sentiment as a purifying and redeeming influence, and in the next breath proclaim that the sole way to avert the ruin now menacing the world is to guarantee to all nations freedom to develop, "unhindered, unthreatened, unafraid." So, forsooth, are we to end war. Nature laughs at such dreams. The life of one is the death of another. Where are the teeming populations of the West Indies, where the civilisations of Mexico or of Peru, where are the blackfellows of Australia? Since means of subsistence are limited, the fancy that one group can increase or develop save at the expense of another is an illusion, instantly dissipated by appeal to biological fact, nor would a biologist-statesman look for permanent stability in a multiplication of competing communities, some vigorous, others worthless, but all growing in population. Rather must a people familiar with science see how small and ephemeral a thing is the pride of nations, knowing that both the peace of the world and the progress of civilisation are to be sought not by the hardening of national boundaries but in the substitution of cosmopolitan for national aspiration.

权力可能在法律或者哲学的基础上很好地建立起来，但现代世界迟早会把它们废除。

对于科学，我们已经无视得太久，以至于对于权利和责任，我们只有两种解释，一种源于自然真理，一种来自传统。我们国家公众特别重视的东西，无论是看到刑事法庭上为了公平而导致的残酷结果，还是看到由于社会习俗所要求的医疗道德所导致的绵延的痛苦，或者是审视教育这个问题本身，又或者是任何一个社会生活中的问题，我们其实预见科学会有更明智、更温和的选择。在国家政策这个更广泛的领域里，我们读读政治家的意见，然后耸耸肩膀走开。他们命令我们提升民族气质，来消除上述问题的影响，在下一秒钟又宣称，要避免世界受到毁灭性的威胁，唯一的办法就是保证所有国家自由发展，"不受阻碍，不受威胁，不再害怕"。这样，我们绝对可以结束战争。自然也会嘲笑这样的梦想。一种生命的开始，就是另一种生命的结束。西印度群岛稠密的人口现在哪儿去了？古墨西哥文明和秘鲁文明现在又如何？澳大利亚的黑人又到哪儿去了？因为生活资料是有限的，那种一个群体的发展不会消耗另一个群体的资源的想法只是一个幻想，生物学事实也会马上打破这个幻想。一个懂生物的政治家也不会在一个不断增长的竞争激烈的群落中寻求永久的稳定，有些人充满活力，有些人毫无价值，但这两种人都会不断增加。一个深谙科学的人会理性地发现，民族的骄傲是多么微不足道，多么短暂易逝，而世界的和平和文明的进步，不能靠加强边防线就能巩固，不能靠修建大都市就能加强，只有提升一个民族的抱负才能获得。

通过学校的比赛，可以锻炼一个人的勇气、忍耐力、自控力、合作精神、公平竞争意识和领导才能。

——F.B.麦林

ATHLETICS

By F.B. MALIM
Master of Haileybury College [①]

At a conference held by the Froebel Society [②] in January, 1917, the subject for discussion was the employment of women teachers in boys' schools. With some of the questions considered, whether women should have shorter hours than men, whether they are capable of enforcing discipline, and the like, I am not now concerned; but I was interested to hear from one speaker after another that a woman was at a real disadvantage in a boys' school, because she could not take part in the games. The speakers did not come from the public schools [③], whose devotion to athletics constitutes, we are sometimes told, a public danger, but mainly from primary and secondary day schools [④] in London. But none the less it was assumed that a boy's games are an essential part of his education. The same assumption is made by the managers of boys' clubs and similar organisations which are endeavouring to carry on the education of boys who have left the elementary schools at the age of fourteen. In spite of the great difficulty of finding grounds to play on in the neighbourhood of great towns, cricket and football are encouraged by any possible means among the

---

① Haileybury College：黑利伯瑞学校，是一所享有盛誉的男子中学，位于澳大利亚墨尔本东南近郊，占地 100 公顷。学校成立于 1892 年，多年来为澳大利亚培养了不少领导人才，教学水平在澳大利亚名列前茅。

② Froebel Society：弗勒贝尔协会。弗勒贝尔（1782~1852），德国教育家，幼儿园创始人。

③ public school：公学，英国私立贵族中学，最早成立于 14~15 世纪，分为男校和女校，以伊顿和哈罗最为有名。

④ day school：日校，非寄宿制学校。

论体育

F. B. 麦林

黑利伯瑞学校校长

1917年1月，在弗勒贝尔协会主办的一个会议上，大家讨论的主题是男校是否应该雇用女性教师。有些问题，比如：女教师的工作时间是不是应该短点儿，她们是否有能力管教学生、执行纪律，等等，我现在倒不关心了，我很感兴趣的是，一个又一个的发言者都提到，女性在男校的一个真正不便之处，在于她们不能上体育课。尽管有人说公学对体育的热爱已经成了一种公共危险，但说这话的人却不是来自公学，而主要来自伦敦的中小学。的确，体育比赛已经成为中小学生教育的一个基本部分。抱着同样想法的还有男生俱乐部和类似组织的管理者，这些组织在男生14岁小学毕业后，努力让他们继续接受这方面的教育。虽然在城镇的社区中要找到踢球的场地非常困难，但这些在工业中心工作的年轻人，仍然想尽办法打打板球、踢踢足球。而对英国学生来说，体育比赛已经越来越成为教育的一部分，那些负责他们成长环境的人有义务为他们提供和组织比赛。这的确是一个现代化的进步。我听到一个很早在马尔伯勒学校读过书的人说，那时候学校不会为打板球的学生提供任何装备，学生们要自己赞助

working lads of our industrial centres. Games are more and more being regarded as a desirable element in the education of the British boy, and are provided for him and organised for him by those responsible for his environment. But this is quite a modern development. I have been told by one who was at Marlborough [①] in the very early days of that school, that so far were the authorities from providing any means of playing cricket, that the boys themselves were obliged to subscribe small sums for the purchase of the necessary material. The book containing the names of the subscribers fell into the hands of the head master, who gated for the term all boys on the list, assuming without inquiry that they were the clients of a juvenile bookmaker.

When we ask why we have come to regard games as a part of a boy's education, we shall naturally answer first that a full education is concerned with the proper development of the body. For this purpose we may employ the old fashioned gymnastic exercises, the modern Swedish exercises or outdoor games. And of these the greatest is games. "So far," says Dr. Saleeby, "as true race culture is concerned, we should regard our muscles merely as servants or instruments of the will. Since we have learnt to employ external forces for our purposes, the mere bulk of a muscle is now a matter of little importance. Of the utmost importance, on the other hand, is the power to coordinate and graduate the activity of our muscles, so that they may become highly trained servants. This is a matter however not of muscle at all, but of nervous education. Its foundation cannot be laid by mechanical things, like dumb-bells and exercises, but by games in which will and purpose and co-ordination are incessantly employed. In other words the only physical culture worth talking about is nervous culture. The principles here laid down are daily defied in very large measure in our nurseries, our schools and our barrack yards. The play of a child, spontaneous and purposeful, is supremely human and characteristic. Although when considered from the outside, it is simply a means of muscular development, properly considered it is really the means of nervous development. Here we see muscles used as human muscles should be used, as instruments of mind. In schools the same principles should be

---

① Marlborough：此处应指 Marlborough College，马尔伯勒学校，创办于 1843 年，建校之初只招收英国各教堂牧师的儿子，1968 年开始招收女生，现为一所男女合校的私立寄宿学校，招收 13~18 岁的学生。

一些钱来购买必要的物品。赞助的方式是购书，印有赞助人名字的书会落到校长手中，以便他察看本学期是否所有的学生都在名单上，以确认学生都从一个青年书商处购了书。

当问到为什么认为体育比赛是男生教育中必不可少的一部分时，我们会很自然地回答，全面的教育离不开适当的身体锻炼。为了这个目的，我们会做旧式体操、现代瑞典体操，或者户外运动。在这些运动中，最伟大的是竞技体育。"目前为止，"塞利比博士说，"就真正的竞技文化而言，肌肉应该仅仅是意志的仆人或者工具。自从我们学会了运用外部力量来实现我们的目的，肌肉的力量就不太重要了。从另一方面来说，最重要的是如何协调和管理肌肉的活动，让它们更好地为我们服务。这个过程和肌肉已经没有关系了，这是神经的问题。这个过程的基础不能通过机械的锻炼——比如哑铃和体操训练——获得，而是要通过竞技比赛才能提升，因为在比赛中，意志和合作更为重要。换句话说，唯一值得讨论的身体文化就是神经文化。而神经文化中的原则，在幼儿园、学校和家中后院里，很大程度上都被否决了。儿童的玩耍，无论是自发的还是有目的性的，是最具有人性、最具有特点的。虽然从外部来看，玩耍只是肌肉发展的方式，但其实也是神经发展的一种方式。学校也应该认识到这种原则。无论是从生理还是心理的角度而言，赛场都远远胜过体育馆。"

低估瑞典式的体育锻炼肯定是一个错误。这种锻炼的目的不在于单方面地锻炼肌肉，而是锻造一个健康、灵敏而又协调发展的身体。在过去的三年中，军事部门就遇到了不少问题，不少人因为不断重复相同的体力活动而导致肌肉单方面发展，或者由于长期坐在办公桌前

recognised. From the biological and psychological point of view, the playing field is immensely superior to the gymnasium."

It would be a mistake to under-estimate the value of the Swedish system of physical exercises. Its object is not the abnormal development of muscle, but the production of a healthy, alert and well balanced body. The military authorities in the last three years have been confronted with the problem of restoring promptness of movement, erectness of carriage, poise and flexibility to numbers of men whose muscles have been given a one-sided development by the constant performance of one kind of manual work, or have grown flabby by long sitting at a desk, and the task would have been much less successfully tackled without the aid of the Swedish methods. In schools these exercises may be used with real benefit given two conditions, small classes and a really skilled instructor. For the value a boy derives from the exercises, to a very large extent depends upon himself, on the concentration of his own will. It is almost impossible to make sure in a large class that this concentration is given, and any kind of exercise done without purpose or resolution rapidly degenerates into the most useless gesticulations. But though we may use physical exercises as an aid, I should be sorry to see them ever regarded as a substitute for games. Even supposing that they were an adequate substitute in the development of the body (which I doubt) they cannot claim to have an effect at all comparable to that of games in the development of character. Sometimes the most extravagant claims are put forward on behalf of athletics as a school of character, almost as extravagant as are the terms in which at other times the "brutal athlete" is denounced. I don't think it is found by experience that athletes cherish higher ideals or are more humble-minded than their less muscular fellows; I doubt if they become more charitable in their judgments or more liberal in their giving. We must carefully limit the claims we make, and then we shall find that we have surer grounds to go on. What virtues can we reasonably suppose to be developed by games? First I should put physical courage. It certainly requires courage to collar a fast and heavy opponent at football, to fall on the ball at the feet of a charging pack or to stand up to fast bowling on a bumpy wicket. Schoolboy opinion is rightly intolerant of a "funk," and we should not attach too

而导致肌肉松弛等，如何帮助他们恢复原有的速度、体态、平衡和灵活性是个很难处理的问题。如果没有瑞典体操的协助，这些问题不会解决得那么成功。在学校里，如果具备两个条件：一是小班教学，二是有一个擅长体操的老师，那么这些锻炼也会真正有益。一个学生能否从锻炼中受益，主要取决于自身是否能专注其中。在一个大班里，学生很难完全集中精力，任何一项锻炼，没有决心去做，不久就会沦为一种无用的动作。虽然我们可以把锻炼作为一种协助，但它很难取代比赛。即使体操在身体发展方面可以完全替代比赛（我对此持怀疑态度），但它在培养性格方面是完全难以和比赛相比的。有时候，甚至有人会夸张地提出竞技精神代表了一种性格，就像"粗鲁的运动员"这个术语在其他时候也会被批评一样。有的观点认为，运动员有更高的理想，比其他肌肉不那么发达的人更谦虚。我不认为这种观点是经验之谈，我甚至怀疑运动员是否会在判断方面更为仁慈，在付出的时候更为大方。我们在做出声明的时候一定要谨慎，这样才能踏踏实实地继续讨论。那么竞技体育究竟能带来什么样的优良品德呢？首先，我认为是勇敢。只有勇敢的人，才敢在足球场上抱住一个飞奔的沉重对手，压上一群人脚下的球，或者站起来飞快地扑到球门上。小学生是不能容忍胆小鬼的，我们也应当重视这种男子汉的美德，把其放在首要位置。考虑到要在这个国家发展的美德，我们发现，为了国家安全，培养年轻人的勇气是必不可少的。在英格兰的下一代身上，已经具备了这种品质，这可以从弗兰德的球场和卡利珀洛的海滩上得到证明。因此，我们不用理会那些谴责有些比赛很危险的人。众所周知，那些值得我们获取的东西，很少有不经过艰苦努力就可得到的，同样，有些东西甚至要冒着风险才能获得。对孩子而言，没有什么比

small a value to this first of the manly virtues. Considering as we must the virtues which we are to develop in a nation, we realise that for the security of the nation courage in her young men is indispensable. That it has been bred in the sons of England is attested by the fields of Flanders and the beaches of Gallipoli. We shall therefore give no heed to those who decry the danger of some schoolboy games. For we shall remember that just as few things that are worth gaining can be won without toil, so there are some things which can only be won by taking risks. Few things are less attractive in a boy than the habit of playing for safety; in the old prudence is natural and perhaps admirable, in the young it is precocious and unlovely. But we need not introduce unnecessary risk by the matching of boys of unequal size and age. The practice, for example, of house games [①] in which the boys of one house play together, without regard to size or skill, is very much inferior to an organisation of games by means of "sets," graded solely by the proficiency which boys have shown. In each set boys are matched with others whose skill approximates to their own; they are not overpowered by the strength of older boys and can get the proper enjoyment from the display of such skill as they possess.

And as we desire our games to foster the spirit that faces danger, so we shall wish them to foster the spirit that faces hardship, the spirit of endurance. That is why I think that golf and lawn tennis are not fit school games; they are not painful enough. I am afraid we ought on the same ground to let racquets go, though for training in alertness and sheer skill, in the nice harmony of eye and hand racquets has no equal. But cricket, football, hockey, fives can all be painful enough; often victory is only to be won by a clinching of the teeth and the sternest resolve to "stick to it" in face of exhaustion. This is the merit of two forms of athletics which have been oftenest the subject of attack, rowing and running. Both of course should be carefully watched by the school doctor; for both careful training is necessary. But a sport which encourages boys to deny themselves luxuries, to scorn ease, to conquer bodily weariness by the exercise of the will, is not one which should be banished because for some the spirit has triumphed to the hurt of the flesh. In a self-indulgent age when sometimes it

---

① house games：此处可能是指 20 世纪初在英国流行的室内游戏室，内有各种设施，儿童可以在其中玩过家家等游戏。

玩得安全更无趣了。对老年人来说，谨慎是自然而可取的；对年轻人而言，谨慎就有点早熟和讨嫌了。但是，我们也不必把不同岁数、不同体格的男生放在一起比赛，以免带来不必要的风险。例如，在游戏室做游戏的时候，一个房间的男生一起玩，而不考虑游戏规模和技巧，就远远不如按照级别来组织游戏，也就是按照他们对游戏的熟练度来组织，更有意思。在每一个级别当中，男生和他们技巧接近的人比赛，这样他们既不会被年龄稍大的孩子的力量吓倒，也能从他们所展示的技巧中获得游戏的快乐。

正如我们希望体育比赛能锻炼直面危险的精神，我们也希望体育比赛还能锻炼直面困难的精神和忍耐的精神。这也是为什么我认为高尔夫和草地网球不适合学校体育比赛——它们的对抗程度不够。基于同样的原因，恐怕壁球也要靠边站，虽说在训练灵敏度和纯技巧方面，在训练眼睛的协调性方面，壁球的作用无出其右者。但是板球、足球、曲棍球、手球才足以锻炼一个人，在这些运动中想要获得胜利，必须在筋疲力尽的时候，也要咬紧牙关，用最坚忍的意志坚持到最后。这就是两种不同类型的运动各自的优点，这两类运动都包含了很多攻击、翻滚和跑步动作。当然进行这两种运动都要由校医陪伴，两者都需要认真训练。但是如果一项运动能鼓励学生通过意志的锻炼来克服享乐主义，蔑视轻易获得，战胜身体上的疲惫，这种运动绝不能取消，因为精神战胜了肉体上的痛苦。在一个自我放纵的时代，有时候对手的嘲笑似乎是真实的，最具有英国特色的词似乎是"舒适"，那么在学校里保留一些完全排斥舒适的运动，绝对是大有益处的。

再次强调，如果一个学生没有学会克制脾气，那

has seemed that the gibe of our enemies is true, that the most characteristic English word is "comfort," it is good to retain in our schools some forms of activity in which comfort is never considered at all. The Ithaca which was [Greek: hagathê koyrotrophos] was also [Greek: trêcheia].

Again no boy can meet with real athletic success who has not learnt to control his temper. It is not merely that public opinion despises the man who is a bad loser; but that to lose your temper very often means to lose the game. It may be true that a Rugby forward does not develop his finest game until an opponent's elbow has met his nose and given an extra spice to his onslaught. But in the majority of contests the man who keeps his head will win. Notably this is true in boxing, a fine instrument of education, whatever may be the objections to the prize ring. So dispassionate a scientist as Professor Hall in his monumental work on *Adolescence*, describes boxing as "a manly art, a superb school for quickness of eye and hand, decision, full of will and self-control. The moment this is lost, stinging punishment follows. Hence it is the surest of all cures for excessive irascibility, and has been found to have a most beneficial effect upon a peevish or unmanly disposition."

But perhaps the best lesson that a boy can learn from his games, is the lesson that he must play for his side and not for himself. He does not always learn it; the cricketer who plays for his average, the three-quarters who tries to score himself, are not unknown, though boyish opinion rightly condemns them. Popular school ethics are thoroughly sound on this point, and it is the virtue of inter-school and inter-house competitions, that in them a boy learns what it is to forget self and to think of a cause. There is a society outside himself which has its claim upon him, whose victory is his victory, whose defeat is his defeat. Whether victory comes through him or through another, is nothing so long as victory be won; later in life men may play games for their health's sake or for enjoyment, but they lose that thrill of intense patriotism, the more intense because of the smallness of the society that arouses it, with which they battled in the mud of some November day for the honour of their school or house. Small wonder that when school-fellows meet after years of separation, the memories to which they most gladly return, are the memories of hard-won victories and manfully contested defeats.

么他绝对不可能真正获得比赛的胜利。这不仅因为大家瞧不起坏脾气的输家，而且因为一个人越容易发脾气，就越容易输掉比赛。的确，一个勇往直前的橄榄球队员在被对手一胳膊打到鼻子之后，可能会发挥得更好，反而可能给他的进攻增添色彩。但在大部分比赛中，头脑冷静才会获胜。拳击比赛尤其如此，虽然很多人反对这项比赛，但拳击是很好的教育工具。所以，即使像霍尔教授这么冷静的科学家，在他不朽的著作《论青春》中，也把拳击描述为"一项男人的艺术，一所锻炼眼睛和手、锻炼杀伐决断、锻炼意志和自控力的超级学校。这一秒钟失手，下一秒就会被惩罚。因此，拳击是治疗脾气暴躁最可靠的方法，能最有效地改善一个人的急躁性格"。

但也许一个男生可以从比赛中学到的最好的一课，就是他必须为团队比赛，而非为个人比赛。并非每个人都能学会这一点，总有板球手在场上敷衍了事，中后卫只为自己得分，在小男孩看来，这些做法也是应该谴责的。好在一般学校的道德观在这一点上都很健康，正是不同学校和不同球队之间的竞争，才使一个男生学会忘记自己，而为了一项事业努力。这种竞争让他认识到，在他之外有一个社会，他对这个社会负有责任，社会的胜利就是他的胜利，社会的失败就是他的失败。不论胜利是由他还是由其他人赢得的，都没有关系。在以后的人生中，他可能会为了健康、为了乐趣而竞争，但这些都再也没有那种强烈的爱国主义一般的激动之情了。可能他在十一月的泥泞中奋战，只不过是为了捍卫学校或者社团的荣誉。这种小时候的比赛涉及的社会范围很小，因而更让人激动。难怪分别经年后再相遇的同学，最喜欢回忆的就是那些经过艰苦取得的胜利和虽败犹荣的赛事。

But victory must be won by fair means. There is a story (possibly without historical foundation) that a foreign visitor to Oxford said that the thing that struck him most in that great university was the fact that there were 3000 men there who would rather lose a game than win it by unfair means. It would be absurd to pretend that that spirit is universal: the commercial organisation of professional football and the development of betting have gone a long way to degrade a noble sport. But the standard of fair play in school games is high, and it is the encouragement of this spirit by cricket and football that renders them so valuable an aid in the activities of boys' clubs in artisan districts. It has been argued that the prevalence of this generous temper among our troops has been a real handicap in war; that we have too much regarded hostilities as a game in which there were certain rules to be observed, and that when we found ourselves matched against a foe whose object was to win by any means, fair or foul, the soldiers who were fettered by the scruples of honour were necessarily inferior to their unscrupulous foe. It has perhaps yet to be proved that in the long run the unchivalrous fighter always wins, and I doubt whether any of us would really prefer that even in war we should set aside the scruples of fair play. But in the arts and pursuits of peace that man is best equipped to play a noble part who realises that there are rules in the great game of life which an honourable man will respect, that there are advantages which he must not take. How often does some rather inarticulate hero, who has refused some tempting prospect or spurned some specious offer, explain his act of self-denial by the simple phrase of his boyhood, "I thought it wasn't quite playing the game." Schoolboy honour is not always a faultless thing; sometimes it means the hiding of real iniquity. But the honour of the playing field is a generous code, and to have learnt its rules is to have learnt the best that the public opinion of a boy community can teach.

The chairman of a great engineering firm recently told the Incorporated Association of Headmasters, that when he went to Oxford to get recruits for his firm, he did not look for men who had got a First in Greats, but for men who would have got a First, if they had worked. For these men had probably given a good deal of their time to

但胜利必须通过公平的方式获得。有个故事（可能
没有历史依据）讲到，一个参观牛津大学的外国游客说，
这所大学最打动他的，是学校里有3000人宁愿输掉比
赛，也不愿意通过不公平的方式获胜。如果我们假装认
为在社会中这种公平竞争的精神已经很普遍，则会显得
很可笑：职业足球的商业化组织和赌球的发展早就开始
腐蚀这项高尚的运动。但在学校比赛中，公平竞争的精
神还是贯彻得很好，也正是板球和足球对公平竞争的推
崇，才使得这两项运动成为在手工艺人集中的地区男孩
俱乐部最具锻炼价值的活动。有人认为，这种慷慨的气
质在军队中流行已经成为打仗的阻碍；他们认为我们早
已把战争看作一场比赛，而战争同样要遵守一定的规则。
在战争中我们发现对手为了获得胜利可以不择手段，而
我们的士兵却仍然因为尊严而有所顾忌，很可能不是毫
无顾忌的敌人的对手。下面这一点也许还有待证明，那
就是从长远来看放弃骑士精神的战士总会胜利，但我怀
疑并不是所有人都发自内心地认为，在战争中我们应该
全然不顾公平竞争的原则。在艺术和追寻和平的过程中，
人们已经做好了充分的准备来发挥自己高尚的一面，因
为他们意识到，在生命这场伟大游戏中，一个有尊严的
人必须遵守某些规则，必须放弃某些利益和好处。经常
会有一些不善言辞的英雄，在拒绝了某些诱人的前景或
者看上去很美的提议后，解释说，他的拒绝只不过是因
为童年时期的教育："我觉得这不符合游戏规则。"学生式
的荣誉感并非完美无瑕，有时候它可能意味着掩盖罪恶。
但是赛场上的尊严是慷慨正义的代名词，学会公平竞争
的规则是公众舆论对一个儿童最好的教育。

一个大公司的董事长最近告诉校长联合会，他到牛
津为公司招人的时候，不会招在学位考试中考第一的
学生，而是招收如果努力学习可能会获得第一的学生。

rowing or games and had thereby learnt something of the art of dealing with men. The student who sticks to his books learns many lessons, but not this. To be captain of a house or of a school, and to do it well is to practise the art of governing on a small scale. A sore temptation to the schoolmaster is to interfere too much in school games. He sees obvious mistakes being made, wrong tactics being adopted, the wrong sides chosen, and he longs to interfere. He is anxious for victories, and forgets that after all victories are a very secondary business, that games are only a means, not an end, that if he does not let the boys really govern and make their mistakes, the game is failing to provide the training that it ought to give. It is undoubted that schools which are carefully coached by competent players, where the responsibility is largely taken out of the captain's hands, are more likely to win their matches. But much is lost, though the game may be won. The strong captain who goes his own way, chooses his own side, frames his own tactics and inspires the whole team with his own spirit, has had a practical training in the management of men which will stand him in good stead in the greater affairs of life. "We are not very well satisfied" said a War Office official, "with the stamp of young officer we are getting. Many of them never seem to have played a game in their lives, though they are first-rate mathematicians." And there is no doubt that whether for war or peace mathematics is not a substitute for leadership.

Courage, endurance, self-control, public spirit, fair play, leadership, these are the virtues which we find may be encouraged by the practice of games at school. It is not a complete list of the Christian virtues, perhaps rather we might call them Pagan virtues, but it is a fine list for all that. And the best of it is that they are as it were unconsciously learnt, acquired by practice, not by inculcation. The boy who follows virtue for its own sake would be, I fear, a sad prig, but the boy who follows a football for the sake of his house, may develop virtue and enjoy the process.

But what are we to put on the other side of the account? If it be true that athletics is a fine school for character, what is the ground for the frequent complaint that the public schools make a "fetish" of athleticism? What precisely is the complaint? It is this, that boys regard, and are encouraged to regard their games as the most important

因为这些学生也许把很多时间放在赛艇或者其他比赛上了，在那些活动中，他们能够学会和人相处的艺术。把时间花在书本上的学生可能学会了很多知识，但学不到这些。成为一个机构和一所学校的领导，要做得好的话，需要"放手"的艺术。作为一个学校的校长，会不由自主对学校比赛插手过多。如果他发现有人犯了明显的错误，有人实施了错误的策略，有人做了错误的选择，然后他就想插手了。他想获得胜利，因而忘记了胜利本身不是最重要的，比赛只是一种手段，不是目的，如果不让学生自己主宰、自己犯错，比赛就失去了本身的意义。毫无疑问，如果学校的球队有能干的球员认真执教，责任也并非主要在队长手中，这样的队伍更容易获胜。但虽然比赛赢了，失去的其实更多。一个强势的球队队长，会有自己的方法、自己的决定和自己的战略，并用自己的精神鼓励整个队伍，用实用的训练管理他的队员，这对他以后的人生有很大帮助。"我们对年轻军官的性情不是很满意。"一位陆军部官员说，"很多人好像从来没有打过一场比赛，虽说他们是一流的数学家。"毫无疑问，无论是在战时还是在和平时期，数学才能都不能取代领导才能。

学校的比赛，可以锻炼一个人的勇气、忍耐力、自控力、合作精神、公平竞争意识和领导才能。这当然不是一个基督徒应有的所有美德，但我们也许可以把它们视为一个异教徒应该具有的全部美德。最让人称道的是这些美德是通过实践下意识学会的，而非由老师灌输的。一个为了学习美德而学习美德的学生，不过是假正经，但一个为了自己学校而遵守球赛规则的学生，会培养出这些美德，并享受学习的过程。

但是如果我们站在这个问题的另一面，结果会怎样呢？如果竞技体育的确是一所培养性格的好学校，为什

side of their school life, that their interest in them is so overpowering that they have no interest left for the development of the intellect or the acquisition of knowledge, that prominent athletes, not brilliant scholars, are the heroes of a boy community, and that in consequence many men of the better nourished classes, after they have left school, look upon their amusements as the main business of life, give to them the industry and concentration which should be bestowed upon science, letters or industry, and swell the ranks of the amiable and incompetent amateur. It is argued that schools are converted into pleasant athletic clubs, and that boys, instead of learning there to work, merely learn to play. Now this is a serious indictment; it is a good thing to learn to play, but it is not the only thing a school should teach. Riding, shooting and speaking the truth may have been an adequate curriculum for an ancient Persian, but it would not provide a sufficient equipment to enable a man to face the stress of modern competition, or to understand the developments of the science and industry of to-day.

Is too much time given to the playing of games? In winter time I should say No. I suppose that if we include teaching hours and preparation, a boy spends some six hours a day on his intellectual work, or if you prefer, he is supposed to spend that time. A game of football two or three times a week, does not last more than an hour and a quarter; if you add a liberal allowance for changing and baths, two hours is the whole time occupied. A game of fives or a physical drill class need not demand more than an hour. The game that really wastes time—and I am sorry to admit it—is cricket. I am not thinking so much of the long waits in the pavilion when two batsmen on a side are well set, and the rest have nothing to do but to applaud. I see no way out of that difficulty, so long as wickets are prepared as they are now by artistic groundsmen. I am thinking rather of the excessive practice at nets. An enthusiastic house captain is apt to believe that by assiduous practice the most unlikely and awkward recruit can be converted into a useful batsman, and the result is that he will drive all his house day after day to the nets, until they begin to loathe the sight of a cricket ball.

We should recognise that cricket is a game for the few; the majority of boys can

么经常有人抱怨说学校过于依赖体育比赛了？这些抱怨究竟是怎么回事？答案是，学生认为——同时学校也鼓励学生这样认为，体育比赛是他们校园生活中最重要的部分，结果他们在这方面的兴趣压倒一切，甚至没有兴趣发展才智、学习知识了。在学生群体中，著名运动员而非杰出学者才是他们的英雄，随之而来的是，在那些精心培育的班级中，很多学生在课后把体育娱乐当作生活中的大事，把本来应该放在科学、文学或者其他方向的精力放在体育娱乐上，最后把自己变成了不同程度的业余体育爱好者，和蔼可亲，却水平不高。有人说，学校已经变成了舒适的体育俱乐部，学生们在学校里学的不是如何学习，而是如何玩耍。这是一个严重的警告。学习玩耍是件好事，但一所学校绝对不应该仅仅教授这些东西。学习骑马、射击和说真话对一个古代波斯人来说可能是一份完善的学习计划，但这对一个要学习如何面对现代竞争压力、理解当今科学和工业发展的人来说，是远远不够的。

我们真的把太多时间花在体育比赛上了吗？我的答案是：至少在冬天没有。如果我们把教学时间和预习时间加起来，一个学生一天在功课上大概要花 6 个小时，或者说，他应该花 6 个小时。而一周两三场足球比赛，平均一天不会超过一小时一刻钟，即使把换衣服和洗澡的时间加上，最多也不会超过两个小时。一场手球赛或体能训练课最多只要一个小时。真正浪费时间的运动——我很抱歉地承认——是板球。当一个队中两个板球击球手定下来以后，其他人无事可做，只能鼓掌，更不用说选手席上其他板凳队员了。只要球门被守门员看好了，我觉得基本没有办法走出这种困境。我更为顾虑的是过度的网前训练。一个热忱的队长往往认为，通过艰苦的练习，最笨拙的新手也可以变成一个有用的投手，

never make good cricketers. And happy are those schools which are near a river and can provide an alternative exercise in the summer, which does not require exceptional quickness of eye and wrist and does provide a splendid discipline of body and spirit. In the summer it is well to exempt all boys from cricket, who have really a taste for natural history or photography. Summer half-holidays are emphatically the time for hobbies, and it is a serious charge against our games if they are organised to such a pitch that hobbies are practically prohibited. The zealous captain will object that such "slacking" is destroying the spirit of the house. We must endeavour to point out to him that the unwilling player never makes a good player, and that such a boy may be finding his proper development in the pursuit of butterflies, a development which he would never gain by unsuccessful and involuntary cricket. House masters too are apt to complain that freedom for hobbies is subversive of discipline, and to quote the old adage about Satan and idle hands. That there is risk, is not to be denied. But you cannot run a school without taking risks. Our whole system of leaving the government largely in the hands of boys is full of risks. Sometimes it brings shipwreck; more often it does not. For in the majority of cases the policy of confidence is justified by results.

There is one way of wasting time that is heartily to be condemned, the waste involved in looking on. I am inclined to think that if all athletic contests took place without a ring of spectators, we should get all the good of games and very little of the evil. Certainly professional football would lose its blacker sides if there were no gate money and no betting. Few men or boys are the worse for playing games; it is the applause of the mob that turns their heads. But I am afraid I am not logical enough to say that I would forbid boys to watch matches against another school; the emotions that lead to the "breathless hush in the Close" are so compounded of patriotism and jealousy for the honour of the school, that they are far from ignoble. But I would not have boys compelled to watch the games against clubs and other non-school teams. Above all, if they watch, they must have a run or a game to stir their own blood. The half-holiday must not be spent in shivering on a touchline and then crowding round a fire.

他必须做的就是日复一日地把所有队员拉到网前，直到他们一看到板球就厌恶为止。

我们应当认识到板球是少数人的运动，大部分男生难以成为优秀的板球手。那些离河较近的学校应该感到幸运，因为在夏天这些学校可以有其他的替代运动，这些运动不需要眼疾手快，但确实能极大地锻炼身体和意志。在夏天让所有学生从板球运动中解放出来是相当不错的，学生们可以培养对自然历史和摄影的品味。暑假显然是发展业余爱好的好时候，如果只允许学生进行体育比赛，而几乎禁止了其他业余爱好，肯定会遭人谴责。一个充满激情的队长可能会反对这种"惰性"，认为它会毁掉队伍的精神。但我们必须尽力向他指出，一个勉强而为的队员不会成为一个好队员，而一个男孩可能在抓蝴蝶的时候，忽然发现他想要的东西，而这种东西在既不成功也不情愿的板球运动中永远也不会被发现。球队的老板也会抱怨其他爱好的自由发展可能会毁掉纪律，并引用有关撒旦和懒人的谚语来证明。无可否认，这样一定会有风险。但管理一个学校就一定会冒风险。我们把学校的管理权主要放在学生手中的体系本身就充满了风险。有时候，可能会船毁人亡，但大多数情况下，不会这样。因为大多数情况下，结果都证明我们对学生的信任是有道理的。

有一种浪费时间的方式必须受到谴责，那就是把时间浪费在观看上。我认为如果所有的体育比赛都没有人围观，我们更能从中受益，同时更少受害。如果职业足球比赛没有门票费，没有赌球，那么其负面作用基本能克服。很少有人会因为体育比赛变坏，是那些乌合之众的掌声冲昏了他们的头脑。我会禁止学生观看和其他学校的比赛，因为在"比赛结束时会让人屏住呼吸"，这种混合了爱国主义和高度的学校荣誉感的情绪，显得有点

That the athlete is a school hero and the scholar is not, is most certainly true. The scholar may once in a way reflect glory on the school by success in an examination, but generally he is regarded as a self-regarding person, who is not likely to help to win the matches of the year. But the hero-worship is not undiscriminating; conceit, selfishness, surliness will go far to nullify the influence of physical strength and skill. Boys' admiration for physical prowess is natural and not unhealthy. The harm is done by the advertisement given to such prowess by foolish elders. Foremost among such unwise influences I should put the press. Even modest boys may begin to think their achievements in the field are of public importance when they find their names in print. Some papers publish portraits of prominent players, or a series of articles on "Football at X—" or "The prospects of the Cricket Season at Y—". The suggestion that there is a public which is interested in the features of a schoolboy captain, or wishes to know the methods of training and coaching which have led to the success of a school fifteen, is likely to give boys an entirely exaggerated notion of their own importance and to justify in their minds the dedication of a great deal of time to the successes which receive this kind of public recognition.

Next there is the parent. Our ever active critics are apt to forget that schools are to a large extent mirrors, reflecting the tone and opinion of the homes from which boys come. The parent who says when the boy joins the school, "I do not mind whether he gets in the sixth, but I want to see him in the eleven," is by no means an uncommon parent. I have no objection to his wanting to see his boy in the eleven, the deplorable thing is that he is indifferent to intellectual progress. I have heard an elder brother say, "Tom has not got into his house eleven yet, but he brought home a prize last term. I have written to tell him he must change all that, we can't have him disgracing the family." When a candidate has failed to qualify for admission to the school at the entrance examination, I have had letters of surprised and pained protest, pointing out that Jack is an exceptionally promising cricketer. It is assumed that we should be only too glad to welcome the athlete without regard to his

过于高尚了，当然，我的这种观点可能在逻辑上有点站不住脚。我也不会督促学生观看和其他俱乐部或者非校队的比赛。如果要看，他们首先要热热身或者来场比赛把自己调动起来。半日假不能浪费在为了别人的边线球而激动、围观、争议上。

运动员是学校的英雄，而学者不是，这很可能是真的。学者们可能曾经以这样或那样的方式通过一项考试而给学校带来荣誉，但通常来说，他们都代表的是个人，不会帮助学校获得年度比赛的胜利。而英雄崇拜不是盲目、虚荣而又自私的，坏心眼的人是不会赞扬身体的力量和技巧的。男孩们对于力量的崇拜既自然又健康。害处是那些愚蠢的大人们用广告带来的。在这些不明智的影响中，我最想提到的是媒体。即使是最谦虚的学生，看到他们的名字变成铅字以后，也会开始以为他们在球场上的成就有多重要。有些报纸会刊登主要队员的海报，或者发表一系列名为"X 校的球赛""Y 校的板球季前景"的文章。这种暗示，就是说公众对一个学生队长感兴趣，或者说想知道一个学校球队是靠什么训练和教练方法取得成功的，会给学生们一种放大了的概念——他们很重要，并让他们理所当然地把更多的时间放在这种会得到公众认可的成功中去。

接下来是父母。很多活跃的批评家好像忘了学校在很大程度上就像一面镜子，反映了学生家庭的意见和观点。如果有学生家长说："我不介意他是否能上到高中六年级，但我希望他是校队队员。"这个家长无论如何都很特别；我并不反对他鼓励孩子进入学校球队，可悲的是他对孩子的学业毫不关心。我曾听过一个大一点的孩子说："汤姆根本就没有加入学校球队，但他上学期居然拿回家一个比赛奖。我写信给他说他不能这样做，我们不能接受他这样侮辱他的父母。"当一个学生在入学考试中

standard of work. If we could get the majority of parents to recognise the schoolmaster's point of view, that while games are an important element of education, they are only one element, and that there are others which must not be neglected, we should have made a real step forward towards the elimination of the excessive reverence paid to the athlete.

After the press and the parent comes millinery. Perhaps it is Utopian to suggest that "caps" can be entirely abolished; but the enterprise of haberdashers and the weakness of school authorities have led to a multiplication of blazers, ribbons, caps, jerseys, stockings, badges, scarves and the like, which certainly tend to mark off the successful player from his fellows, and to make him a cynosure of the vulgar and an object of complacent admiration to himself. Success in games should be its own reward. In some cases it certainly is. And the paradox is that very often it is those who are least bountifully endowed by nature who profit most. Some there are who have such natural gifts of strength and dexterity, that from the first they can excel at any game. Triumphs come to them without hard struggle, and they breathe the incense of applause. But others have a clumsier hand, a slower foot, and yet they have a determination to excel, a resolution in sticking to their task that brings them at the last to a fair measure of skill. Such a boy is already rewarded by the toughening of the will that perseverance brings: he does not need a ribbon on his sweater. To give the other, the natural athlete, a coloured scarf, is to run the risk of making him over-value the gifts he owes to nature.

There is no reason why a boy who excels in games should not excel in work. The two are not competing sides of education, they are complementary. The schoolmaster's ideal is that his boys should gain the advantages of both. The athlete who neglects his work, grows up with a poorly furnished mind and an untrained judgment. The student who neglects his games, grows up without the nervous development that fits his body to be the instrument of his will, and without the knowledge of men and the habit of dealing with men which are indispensable in many callings. It has been proved again and again that it is possible to get the advantages of both these sides of school life. There is no reason

失利，没有获得入学资格的时候，我会收到既惊讶又痛苦的抗议书，说杰克是一个特别有前途的板球手。好像我们应该非常乐意接受一个运动员，而不考虑他的学习成绩。如果我们能让大部分家长接受校长的观点，即竞技体育是教育的一个重要部分，但仅仅是一部分，教育还有其他不可忽视的部分，那我们就在不过分重视体育的道路上前进了一大步。

媒体和父母之后是商家。要想在比赛中完全去掉"球队队帽"可能只是一种幻想，但服饰生产商的勃勃野心和学校当局的弱点联合起来，让比赛中的上衣、饰带、帽子、运动衫、袜子、徽章、丝巾等衣饰不断增加，让成功球员从伙伴中脱离出来，成了庸俗商人的目标，还为此扬扬自得。比赛胜利本身就是一种奖励。有时候，的确是这样。但矛盾的是，很多时候，最没有天赋的人可能获益最多。有些人具有天赋的力量和敏捷身手，从一开始就能在任何比赛中胜出，不用太努力也可以获得胜利，享受热烈的掌声。而其他人手脚较笨拙、缓慢，但他们有获胜的决心、坚持的意志，这些最终会让他们学会良好的技巧。这样的一个学生通过坚持不懈的努力会锻炼出更强韧的意志，而这就是对他的奖赏，他其实不需要球衣上的装饰了。对前一种运动员，即天生的运动员而言，即使是一条彩色的围巾，也可能让他们高估自己的天赋。

在体育比赛中表现优异的学生不可能在学习方面也表现优异，这种看法没有任何道理。这两者不是相互排斥的，而是相互补充的。校长的理想是学生可以从两者的长处中获益。忽视学业的运动员长大以后，头脑通常不太发达，判断力也不够。忽视体育运动的学生，长大以后缺乏神经的训练，难以把身体作为意志的工具，缺乏做人的知识和与人相处的技巧，而这些是完成很多事

why the playing of school games should be anything but a help to the intellectual development of a boy.

But the constant talking about games is by no means harmless, though it is true boys might be talking of worse things. It is related that a French educational critic was once descanting to an English head master on the monotony of the conversation of English public school boys: "They talk of nothing but football." But when he was asked, "And of what do French school boys generally talk?" he was silent. But if "cricket shop" saves us from worse topics, it certainly is destructive of rational conversation on subjects of more general interest. In great boarding schools we collect a population of boys under quite abnormal conditions, cut off for the greater part of their social life from intercourse with older people. It is, I think, a general experience that boys who have been at day schools and are the sons of intelligent parents, have their minds more awakened to the questions of the day in politics, or art, or literature than boys of equal ability who have been at a boarding school. They have had the advantage of hearing their father and his friends discussing topics which are outside the range of school life. Boarding schools are often built in some country place away from the surging life of towns, where the noise of political strife and the roar of the traffic of the world are but dimly heard. In such seclusion the life of the school, particularly the active life of the playing fields, occupies the focus of a boy's consciousness. The geographical conditions tend to narrow the range of his interests, and he remains a boy when others are growing to be men. Those who have the wider tastes, are deterred from talking about them by the ever present fear of "side." They will talk freely to a master of architecture or music or Japanese prints, but they are chary of betraying these enthusiasms to their fellows. And masters are not free from blame: I suppose we all of us sometimes bow down in the house of Rimmon, and when the conversation languishes at the tea-table, fall back on a discussion of the last house match. It is the line of least resistance, and after a strenuous day's work it is not easy to maintain a monologue about Home Rule. Not the least of the boons of the war is that it has ousted games from the foremost place as a topic of conversation.

业必不可少的。大家已经反复证明，在学校中获得这两方面的益处是完全可行的。因此，把参加体育运动看作学生知识发展的一个障碍是完全没有道理的。

虽然学生们可能会谈论更糟糕的东西，但是一直谈论比赛总是不好的。据说，一个法国教育批评家和一个英国校长评论英国公学学生话题很单调的时候说："他们什么都不谈，只谈足球。"但当人家问他："那法国学生一般谈什么？"他不说话了。虽说"板球商店"可能把我们从更糟糕的话题中拯救出来，但这的确也可能阻碍对话往一个更广泛更为理性的方面发展。在"伟大"的寄宿学校里，我们把一群学生集中在一个不太正常的环境中，切断了他们和成年人之间的社会联系。我觉得，如果学生白天上学，回到家接受明智的父母的教育，肯定会比上寄宿学校的学生对于很多问题有更深刻的认识，比如当今政治、艺术、文学，等等。因为他们有机会听到父亲和朋友讨论学校生活以外的东西。在有些国家，寄宿学校常常建在远离喧嚣的城镇生活的地方，这样学生几乎没有机会听到政治争论和外界交通工具的声音。在这样的象牙塔中，学校生活，尤其是比赛场上的生活，就会成为学生意识的焦点。因为地理条件使他们的兴趣范围变得狭隘，当其他人成长为男人的时候，他可能还是一个男孩。那些有着广泛兴趣的人，因为害怕暴露他们的"狭隘"，尽量不谈论这些。他们会自由地讨论建筑、音乐或者日本的绘画大师，但他们会很谨慎地不把他们的热情显露在同伴面前。校方也不是没有责任。我以为我们所有人有时候也忘记了最初的信仰，当我们在茶几旁懒洋洋地谈话的时候，也会谈着谈着就谈到了上一次的比赛。这是最难抗拒的话题，一个人很难在一天的辛勤工作后，继续讨论比如自治之类的严肃话题。战争的一大好处就是终于代替了体育比赛，占据了话题的榜首

I have not noticed that they are less keenly played, although the increase of military work has diminished the time given to them; but they have ceased to monopolise the thoughts of boys. The problem then of reducing the absorption in games is the problem of finding and providing other absorbing interests. We cannot, fortunately, always have the counter-irritant of war. Where we fail now, is that the intellectual training of a boy does not interest him enough in most cases to give him subjects of conversation out of school. We give some few new interests by means of societies, literary, antiquarian or scientific. But the main problem is to make every boy see that the work he does in school is connected with his life, that it is meant to open to him the shut doors around him through which he may go out into all the highways and byways of the world.

Do school games produce the man who regards games as the main business of life? We must emphasise "main." It is certain that they do encourage Englishmen to devote some part of their working life to healthy exercise—and few, I suppose, would wish them to do otherwise. The Indian civilian does not make a worse judge for playing polo, nor is Benin[①] worse administered since golf-links were laid out there. But there are men who never outgrow the boyish narrowness of view that games are the things that matter most. These remain the ruling passion, because no stronger passion comes to drive it out. For this the schools must bear part of the blame, for they have not taught clearly enough that athletics are a means but not an end. Not all the blame, for surely some must rest on a society which tolerates the idler, and has no reproach for the man who says "I live only for hunting and golf." And here as elsewhere, I believe we are judged more by a few failures than by many successes. We can all of us in our experience recall many an honest athlete who is now doing splendid service to Church or State, doughty curates, self-sacrificing doctors, soldiers who are real leaders of men. When they became men they put away childish things, but they have not forgotten what they

---

① Benin: 贝宁, 非洲西部国家, 旧名达荷美。贝宁南濒几内亚湾, 东邻尼日利亚, 北与尼日尔接壤, 西北与布基纳法索相连, 西和多哥接壤, 面积 112,620 平方公里, 首都波多诺伏为国民议会所在地, 科托努则为政府所在地。

位置。虽然我并没有发现学生打比赛打得少些了，因为军事服务占据了他们的时间，使他们减少了运动的时间，至少让比赛不再是唯一占据孩子们思想的东西了。如何降低学生对比赛的兴趣，这其实就是如何找到和提供其他兴趣点的问题。幸运的是，战争只是偶尔为之的其他兴趣。我们现在做得不太成功的是，一个学生的知识训练大多数情况下不能完全吸引他们，让他们在校外也有讨论的主题。我们在社会、文学、考古、科学方面提供的新的东西很少。而主要问题是让每一个学生认识到他在学校的学习和他的生活息息相关，学习意味着为他打开那些关闭的大门，让他有机会迈向世界的各个方向。

学校比赛会不会导致有些学生长大以后把比赛看作人生中最重要的东西呢？这儿我们必须强调"最重要"。确实，它们使英国人把生活中的一部分时间花在健康的运动上，而且我认为几乎没有人会鼓励他们反其道而行之。印度文官不会因为打马球而变成一个糟糕的法官，贝宁也不会因为修了一个高尔夫球场就变得更糟糕。但是，也会有人从来都走不出小男生的狭隘观点，而永远把比赛看作最重要的东西。这种情感一直占据主导地位，是因为没有其他东西来替代。对于这个问题，学校要负一定的责任，因为它们没有教导学生清楚地认识到，体育比赛只是一种手段，而不是目的。毫无疑问，一个社会，如果容忍而不谴责有些懒人的观点"我的生活只是为了打猎和打高尔夫"，那这个社会也应该为此负一部分责任——如果不是全部责任的话。我相信，在很多时候，我们评判一个人，不是看他获得了多少成功，而是盯着那少数几次失败。经验告诉我们，很多诚实的运动员现在兢兢业业地为教堂或者国家服务，是敬业的牧师、高尚的医生、勇敢的战士，他们是真正的领袖。当他们长大以后，他们不再玩孩子气的游戏，但是他们并没有

owe to the discipline of their boyish games. Games are not the first thing in life for them now, but they have no doubt that they can do their work better from an occasional afternoon's play. They see things in their right proportion, because they know that the first thing is to have a job and do it well. If we can teach boys to begin to understand that truth while they are at school, we shall have exorcised the bogey of athleticism. I should expect to find (though I do not know) that the authorities at Osborne and Dartmouth do not need to bother their minds about that bogey. Their boys play games with all a sailor's heartiness, but their ambition is not to be a first-class athlete, but to be a first-class sailor, and the games take their proper place. It may be desirable to reduce the time devoted to games, though as I have said I doubt if there is any need to do so, except for cricket. It may be that we should give more time to handicraft, or military drill. But these things will not change the spirit. What we need to do is to make clearer the object of education in which athletics form a part, that there may be more sense of reality in the boy's school time, more understanding that he is at school to fit himself manfully and capably to play his part on the wider stage of life.

忘记孩子气的游戏在其行为养成中的作用。现在比赛已经不再是生活中的第一要务了，但偶尔在下午打一场球会让他们把工作做得更好。他们认识到不同事情有不同的分量，最重要的是先把工作干好。如果我们在学校里就教会了学生这个道理，我们就已经消除了运动精神的负面影响。我希望（我也不清楚事实）奥斯本和达特茅斯当局不需要为这些方面的影响烦心。他们的学生在比赛的时候像海员一样诚实而热心，而他们的雄心却不是做一个一流的运动员，而是做一个一流的航海员，比赛在他们心中占据了一个合理的位置。减少在比赛上的时间可能有好处，虽然我怀疑我们是否有必要这样做，当然打板球的时间一定要减少。我们也许应该多放点时间在手工、军训上面，但这些东西不会改变实质。我们应该做的是进一步搞清楚教育的目的，体育精神只是教育目的的一部分；在学校生活中培养学生认识现实的精神，让他们理解学习是为了让他们成为真正的男子汉，在更广阔的生活舞台上发挥自己的作用。

健康不仅仅和身体有关，还同时依赖生理和心理活动，依赖从自愿进行的那些活动中得到的享受。

——J.H.拜德里

THE USE OF LEISURE

By J. H. BADLEY
Head Master of Bedales School [①]

To teach a sensible use of leisure, healthy both for mind and body, is by no means the least important part of education. Nor is it by any means the least pressing, or the least difficult, of school problems. "Loafing" at times that have no recognised duties assigned them, is generally a sign of slackness in work and play as well; and if we do not find occupation for thoughts and hands, the rhyme tells us who will. The devils of cruelty and uncleanness will be ready to enter the empty house, and fill it at least with unwholesome talk, and thoughtless if not ill-natured "ragging." Yet work and games, whatever keenness we arouse and encourage in these, cannot fill a boy's whole time and thoughts—or, if they do, his life, whether he is student or athlete, or even the occasional combination of both, is still a narrow one and likely to get narrower as years go by. If life to the uneducated means a soulless round of labour varied by the public-house and the "pictures," so to the half-educated it is apt, except in war time, to mean the office and the club, with interests that do not go beyond golf and

---

①   Bedales School：比得莱斯中学，英国著名私立中学，由 John Badley 创建于 1893 年，迄今已经有 100 多年历史。学校位于英国汉普郡的彼得菲尔德乡村地区，距离伦敦市中心 70 分钟左右的车程。学校占地 120 余英亩，共有学生约 450 人，教职员工 100 余人。此外，该校还设有独立的初中部 Dunhurst（8~13 岁）和学前部 Dunannie（3~8 岁），三所学校全部学生数约 700 人。比得莱斯中学在英国享有盛誉，几乎与伊顿公学等名校齐名。她为英国很多一流大学如剑桥、牛津、帝国大学等每年输送不少生源。英国社会不少名流（尤其是艺术方面的名流）毕业于该学校。

论闲暇

J. H. 拜德里

比得莱斯中学校长

  教育中的一个重要部分，就是教会学生如何明智地利用闲暇时光，这对身体和大脑都有益。这其实也是学校事务中比较急迫和难以处理的一个问题。有时候，无所事事，没有明确的任务，通常是懒散的标志，无论是在工作中还是在玩乐中，都是如此。如果我们自己不给大脑和手脚找点事做，总有人会帮你找。残酷和肮脏这两个魔鬼会乘虚而入，占据我们的头脑和身体，导致我们思想轻率，言语无状，甚至是恶意胡闹。学习和运动，无论在我们的鼓励下可以带来怎样的机敏头脑，都不可能完全占据一个男孩的时间和思想，或者说，如果占据的话，不管是一个学生还是一个运动员，或者两者的结合，他的生活都太狭隘了，而且随着时间会变得越来越狭隘。如果说，生活对于没有受过教育的人来说意味着一场没有灵魂的体力劳动，因为泡酒吧和看电影稍显丰富；而对于受过一些教育的人而言，生活则意味着办公室和俱乐部，他们的兴趣不过就是高尔夫、汽车和桥牌，可能战时情况会有所不同。如果我们的生活空虚、兴趣狭隘，部分原因是来自教育的狭隘和不足，因为这种教育让人至少有一半的能力没有得到发展，一半的兴趣没

motoring and bridge. If our lives are emptier and our interests narrower than they need be, it is partly the result of a narrow and unsatisfying education, which leaves half our powers undeveloped and interests untouched, and too often only succeeds in giving us a distaste for those which it touches. Both for the sake of the present, therefore, to avoid the dangers of unfilled leisure, and still more for the sake of the future, the wise schoolmaster does all he can to foster, in addition to keenness in the regular work and games, interests, both individual and social, of other kinds as well. He will make opportunities for various handicrafts; he will try to stimulate lines of investigation not arranged for in the class-routine; he will encourage the formation of societies both for discussion and active pursuits, for instruction and entertainment. It is the purpose of this essay to suggest what, along these lines, is possible in the school.

But the reasons so far given for the encouragement of leisure-time interests are mainly negative. In order to realise to the full the importance of this side of education, we must look rather at their positive value. From whichever point of view one looks at it, physical, intellectual, or social, this value is not small. Some of these interests contribute directly to health in being outdoor pursuits; and these, in not letting games furnish the only motive and means of exercise, can help to establish habits and motives of no little help in later life, when games are no longer easy to keep up. And even in the years when the call of games is strongest, some rivalry of other outdoor pursuits is useful as a preventive of absorption in athleticism, easily carried to excess at school so as to shut out finer interests and influences. It was a consciousness of this that led Captain Scott [1], in the letter written in those last hours among the Antarctic snows, thinking of his boy at home, and the education that he wished for him, to write: "Make the boy interested in natural history, if you can; it is better than games: they encourage it in some schools."

Besides health—and health, we must remember, is not only a bodily matter, but depends on mental as well as bodily activity, and on the enjoyment of the activity that comes from its being mainly voluntary—the pursuits that we are considering can do much to train skill of various kinds. The class-work represents the minimum that we

---

① Captain Scott: 史考特队长（1868~1912），英国海军军人，南极探险家，1912 年抵达南极，以史考特队长（Captain Scott）之名而享誉。

有得到开发，好不容易开发了也是一团糟。所以，为了避免无聊的闲暇，为了现在，更为了将来，一个聪明的校长在培养学生学习和体育方面的才能的同时，也应该全力以赴地培养学生个人或社会方面的其他兴趣。他应该提供各种手工活动的机会；刺激各种班级日常活动以外的探索；鼓励建立各种社团进行讨论和追求，进行教学和娱乐活动。这篇文章的目的就是讨论在学校里哪些活动是可行的。

　　但是，现在鼓励发展闲暇兴趣的动机都比较消极。为了充分认识教育在这方面的重要性，必须多探讨这些兴趣正面的价值。不论是从哪个方面来看，无论体育、智力，还是社会方面，闲暇兴趣的作用都不小。有些兴趣，如果是户外活动，能直接有利于身体健康，使体育比赛不再是锻炼的唯一手段和目的，同时能帮助一个人形成好的习惯和动机，使其在今后的人生中受益，尤其是在比赛不再容易进行的时候。即使在体育比赛的愿望很强烈的时期，其他户外活动也有利于避免一个人沉迷于比赛之中，特别是有些在学校里过度进行的比赛，很容易把一些更好的兴趣活动拒之门外。正是这种认识让史考特队长在南极圈幸存的最后几个小时，想到了在家的儿子，想到了他所希望带给儿子的教育。他写信说："如果可能的话，培养孩子对自然历史的兴趣吧，这比体育比赛好，有些学校就是这么做的。"

　　我们必须记住，健康不仅仅和身体有关，还同时依赖生理和心理活动，依赖从自愿进行的那些活动中得到的享受。除了健康，我们所考虑的活动也很有利于锻炼各种技能。课堂提供了一个学生必须了解的东西，但还有很多课堂以外的东西同样重要。很多学生在业余兴趣中学到的东西和在课堂中学到的东西一样多。有时候，

expect a boy to know; but there is much that necessarily lies outside it of hardly less value. Many a boy learns as much from the hobby on which he spends his free time as from the work he does in class. Sometimes, indeed, such a free-time hobby reveals the bent that might otherwise have gone undiscovered, and determines the choice of a special line of work for the future career.

But the chief value of such interests lies rather in their influence on other work, and on the general development of character. In giving scope for many kinds of skill, they are helping the intellectual training; and however ready we may be to pay lip-service to the principle of learning by doing, and to admit the educational importance of the hand in brain-development, in most of our school work we still ignore these things, so far as any practical application of them is concerned. One is sometimes tempted to wonder if in the future there may not be so complete a reaction from our present ideas and methods as to make what are now regarded as mere hobbies the main matter of education, and to relegate much of the present school course, as the writing of verses has already been relegated, to the category of optional side-shows. At any rate these free-time interests can supply a very useful stimulus to much of the routine work. In these a boy may find himself for the first time, and discover, despite his experience in class, that he is no fool. Or at least he may find there a centre of interest, otherwise lacking, round which other interests can group, and to which knowledge obtained in various class-subjects can attach itself, and so get for him a meaning and a use. And further, if we do not make the mistake of narrowing the range of choice, and allow, at any rate at first, a succession of interests, the very range and variety of these pursuits is an antidote against the tendency to early specialisation, encouraged by scholarship and entrance examinations, which is one of the dangers against which we need to be on our guard. If, therefore, without mere dissipation of interest, we can widen the range of mental activities and encourage, by discussions, essays, lectures and so forth, reading round and outside the subjects dealt with in class, this is all to the good.

And all this has a social as well as an individual aspect. The meetings for the purposes just mentioned, as well as those for entertainment, have, like games, a real educational value, and do much to cement the comradeship of common interests and common aims that is one of the best things school has to give. And not only among

这种业余时间的兴趣甚至会揭示一个人真正的爱好，并决定一个人一生的职业选择，而这种爱好在其他时候可能很难发现。

但这种兴趣爱好主要的价值，更多地体现在对其他工作和对性格发展的影响上。不同的兴趣爱好能为多种技巧提供发展空间，从而有利于智力发展。无论我们在口头上如何反复强调动手学习的原则，如何承认动手在大脑发展中的重要性，在大部分的学习中，就这些原则的实际应用而言，我们仍然忽视了动手的重要性。我们有时候会忍不住想知道，如果把现在仅仅作为业余爱好的东西当作教育的主业，而忽视目前学校里的很多课程，比如诗歌写作现在已经被忽视了，仅仅成了选修课上的一个点缀，那么将来是不是也不会有一个彻底不同的结果。从任何程度来说，这些业余爱好都可以促进我们的日常工作。在这些爱好中，一个学生可能会第一次发现他也很聪明，尽管课堂上的经验并不能说明这一点，或者他至少会发现一个核心的兴趣，其他兴趣都是围绕着这个兴趣展开的，他所学到不同学科的知识也有了意义和用武之地。更进一步，如果我们不错误地缩小学生兴趣爱好的选择范围，在任何情况下都允许学生继续自己的爱好，那么这种爱好方面的多样化和广泛性可以预防过早的专业化，虽然入学考试和奖学金机制都鼓励这种专业化，但这是我们必须警惕的一个危险。当然，我们最好能不仅仅依赖兴趣就能拓展学生思想活动的范围，并通过讨论、论文和讲座等形式，鼓励学生进行全面的阅读，而不限于课堂上学习的那些科目。

业余活动对个人和社会都有影响。除了上述目的，业余爱好和体育比赛一样，不仅仅有真正的教育价值，而且能极大地加强具有相同爱好和目标的学生之间的友

those of the same age. These are things in which the example and influence of the older are particularly helpful to the younger. They can become, like the games, and perhaps to an even greater extent, one of the interests that help to bind together past and present members of a school. And they afford an opportunity for masters to meet boys on a more personal and friendly footing, and to get the mutual knowledge and respect which are all-important if education is to be, in Thring's[①] definition, a transmission of life through the living to the living. That the organisation of leisure-time pursuits is of the utmost help to the school as well as to the boy, is the unanimous verdict of the schools in which it has long been a tradition. The master who has had charge, for the past five-and-twenty years, of this organisation in one such school writes that there they consider such pursuits as the very life-blood of the school, and the only rational method of maintaining discipline.

If what has here been said is admitted, it is plain that to teach, by every means in our power, the use of leisure, is one of the most important things a school has to do. We might, therefore, turn at once to the consideration of the various means for such teaching that experience has shown to be practicable in the school. But before doing so, there is yet another reason, the most far-reaching of all, to be urged for regarding this as a side of education fully as necessary, at the present time above all, as those sides that none would question. Great as is the direct and immediate value of the interests and occupations thus to be encouraged, their indirect influence is more valuable still, if they teach not only handiness and adaptiveness, but also call forth initiative and individuality, and so help to develop the complete and many-sided human personality which is the crown and purpose of education as of life. We do not now think of education as merely book-learning, nor even as concerned only with mind and body, or only as fitting preparation for skilled work and cultured leisure; but rather as the development of the whole human being, with all his possibilities, interests, and motives, as well as powers, his feelings and imagination no less than reason and will. In a word, education is training for life, with all that this connotes,

---

①　Thring：此处可能指 Edward Thring（1821~1887），英国著名教育家，著名私立寄宿中学阿宾汉姆学校校长。

谊，这是学校能提供的最有意义的东西之一。不仅仅是同龄人之间，学长的经验有时候会对低年级同学特别有帮助。有些兴趣爱好和体育比赛一样，甚至比体育比赛更能把一个学校过去和现在的校友联系起来，让老师们可以从一个更人性、更友好的基础上了解自己的学生。师生之间应相互学习、相互尊重，这一点非常重要，用斯瑞林的定义来说，教育是生活在不同生命之间的一种传递。业余兴趣爱好组织对学校和学生都有极大的帮助，因而在很多学校成为一种传统，也成为评判学校的一个标准。一个在过去的 25 年里一直在这类学校负责组织业余爱好活动的校长写道，他们认为这种追求是一个学校的活力之所在，也是保持学校纪律的一个合理方法。

如果大家都承认上述意见的话，很明显，在我们的能力范围内，通过各种方法教会学生如何处理闲暇时间，是学校要做的最重要的事。所以，我们接下来要考虑的是从以前的经验中找到哪些方法是可行的。但首先，为什么利用闲暇和其他那些毋庸置疑的方面一样是教育中必不可少的一部分？其中还有另外一个原因，一个意义最深远的原因。发展业余兴趣除了立竿见影的作用外，其间接影响也更具价值，特别是如果这些爱好不仅仅鼓励学生的动手能力和适应能力，还鼓励学生的创新能力和个性发展，这些都有利于培养学生全面的个性，这也正是教育乃至生活的意义和目的之所在。我们不认为教育仅仅是读书，不认为教育仅仅关系大脑和身体的发展，也不认为教育仅仅是为了技术工作和文化闲暇做准备。相反，教育为的是一个人全方位的发展，在兴趣、目标、能力、情感、想象力以及理性和意志力各个方面，穷尽一切可能。用一句话来说，教育是生活的训练，正如我们只能在

and, as we learn to live only by living, must be thought of not merely as preparation for life, but as a life itself. Plainly, if we give it a meaning as wide as this, a great part of education lies outside the school, in the influences of the home surroundings and, after school, of occupation and the whole social environment. But during the school years—and they are the most impressionable of all—it is the school life that is for most the chief formative influence; and now more necessarily so than ever. When, a few generations back, life was still, in the main, life in the country, and most things were still made at home or in the village, the most important part of education lay, except for a few, outside the school. Now it is the other way. Town life, the replacing of home-made by factory-made goods, the disappearance of the best part of home life before the demands of industry on the one side and the growth of luxury on the other—these things are signs of a tendency that has swept away most of the practical home-education, and thrown it all upon the school. And the schools have even yet hardly realised the full meaning of this change. Instead of having to provide only a part of education—the specially intellectual and, in the public schools at least, the physical side—we have now to think of the whole nature of the growing boy or girl, and, by the environment and the occupations we provide, to appeal to interests and motives, and give occasion for the right use of powers, that may otherwise be undeveloped or misused. A school cannot now consist merely of class-rooms and playing fields. This is recognised by the addition of laboratories and workshops, gymnasium, swimming-bath, lecture-hall, museum, art-school, music-rooms—all now essentials of a day school as much as of a boarding school. But many of these things are still only partially made use of, and are apt to be regarded rather as ornamental excrescences, to be used by the few who have a special bent that way, at an extra charge, than as an integral part of education for all. All the interests and means of training that they represent, and others as well, need to be brought more into the daily routine; to some extent in place of the too exclusively literary, or at least bookish, training, that has hitherto been the staple of education, but more, perhaps, since it is not possible to include in the regular curriculum *all* that is of value, as optional subjects and free-time occupations, though organised as part of the school course. For

生活中学会生活，这些发展也不仅仅是为生活做准备，而应该当作生活本身。如果我们为闲暇赋予如此广泛的意义，那么教育的很大一部分应该源自学校以外的影响，比如家庭环境的影响，毕业以后则是职业和整个社会的影响。但是在学生时代——这也是最让人容易接受外部影响的时期，学校生活是最能影响一个人发展的因素，现在这个时代尤其如此。在几代人以前，人们主要生活在乡村，大部分东西是自家或者村子里做的，除了极少数人，大部分人的教育主要是在学校以外进行的。而现在，情况正好相反。工厂制造代替了家庭制造，在城镇生活中，一方面是工业化的需要，另一方面是奢侈享受的需要，已经让家庭生活中最好的某些部分消失了。这意味着一个趋势：家庭教育不再可行，教育只能依赖学校。而学校还没有完全了解这个变化的全部意义。学校不仅仅提供一部分教育——特别是智力教育，当然至少在公立学校还包括体育教育，我们现在要思考的是学生的全部特点，以及如何通过学校环境和课程，来引起他们的兴趣，并提供条件让他们健康地发展各种能力。一个学校仅仅拥有教室和操场是不够的，还需要实验室、工作室、体育馆、游泳池、学术厅、博物馆、美术间、音乐室——所有这些现在都是一所日校和寄宿学校的必备设施。但很多设施都没有完全利用起来，而且很大程度上只是一种摆设，而不是教育整体的一部分，只有那些感兴趣的学生才会使用，并且还要额外付费。其实这些设施和其他设施所代表的兴趣都应该成为日常教育的一部分，因为文学训练或者说书本训练，迄今为止仍然被认为是教育的基础，在教育中的位置过于重要，留给其他课程的时间就不多了，而且不可能在常规大纲中包含*所有*有价值的东西，并把这些作为选修课或者课外活

it is not only the few who already know their bent who need opportunity to be made for following it, but rather those who will not discover their powers without practice, or their interests without suggestion or encouragement. In this respect the war has brought opportunities of no little value to the school, not only in the absorbing interest in the war itself and the desire for knowledge and readiness for effort that it awakens, but also in the demands it has made for practical work of many kinds that boys and girls can do, and the lessons of service that it has taught. Work on the land and in the shops, for those whose school time is already too short, is a curtailment, only to be made as a last resort, of the kind of learning they will have no other opportunity to acquire; but it gives to the public schoolboy the feeling of reality that most of his school work lacks. Such opportunities of doing what is seen to be productive and necessary work, are, like the making of things for those at the front, and for the wounded, both in themselves and in the motives that inspire them, a valuable part of education that should not be forgotten when the present need for them is over.

If, then, by the fullest use of leisure occupations, we are, like Canning[①], to call in a new world to redress the balance of the old, what, in actual practice, is possible in the school? For an answer to this question one has only to see what is done in the schools of the Society of Friends[②], in which the use of leisure in these ways has always been a strongly marked feature long before it was taken up by others, with a tradition, indeed, in the older schools, of sixty or a hundred years of accumulated experience behind it. Instead of singling out, for description of the use it makes of leisure, any one school in which it might be supposed that there were special conditions present, it will be best to enumerate the various activities that have long been practised in several different schools. Of those selected for the purpose not all are connected with the Society of Friends; some are for boys and some for girls only, and some co-educational; but alike in being boarding schools, and in keeping their boys

---

① Canning: 此处可能指乔治·坎宁（George Canning），英国杰出的外交家，他一反前任卡斯尔雷子爵的欧洲协调原则，背弃神圣同盟，承认南美各国的解放，自诩用新世界来平衡旧世界。他支持希腊独立运动，1827 年当了 100 天英国首相就病逝于任上。

② Society of Friends: 基督教公谊会，基督教教派，宗教仪式简单且无神职人员，成立于 1660 年左右，反对暴力。

动。因为不仅仅对这些感兴趣的少数学生想有机会在这方面进一步发展，其他人也需要实践来发现自己的才能，需要别人的鼓励和建议来发展自己的兴趣。在这方面，战争给学校带来了相当有价值的机会，不仅仅在于战争对于兴趣的发展，在于战争所唤起的努力和所引起的对知识的渴望，还在于战争需要学生完成的各项实际工作和各种服务。在田间和商店里的工作，对那些本来在学校待的时间就很短的学生来说，虽说进一步缩短了他们的学习时间，也没有其他机会弥补，但同时也给予了他们在学校学习中没有的现实感。这种完成生产活动和实用工作的机会，比如给前线士兵和伤员生产各种用具，本身和从动机上都激励了学生，并成为教育中很有价值一部分，即使现在我们已经不需要这种方式，它的价值也不应该忘记。

如果我们可以像坎宁一样，通过对闲暇活动最充分的利用，在调整旧世界的平衡中引入新的世界，那么学校在实践中会变成什么样呢？要回答这个问题，先来看看基督教公谊会的学校是怎么做的。远在其他学校之前，这类学校对闲暇的充分利用就成为一个突出的特点。在古老一些的学校里，这种传统甚至已经延续了60年或者100年。他们不是挑选出某个具有特殊情况的学校，来规定如何利用闲暇，而是罗列出适合在不同学校长期实践的各种活动。为了这个目的挑选出来的活动，并非都和公谊会有关，有些只适合男生，有些只适合女生，有些则男女生都适合；在寄宿学校也一样，这些活动从男女生很小的时候开始，一直到他们结束中学生涯去上大学或者接受职业培训或者开始工作为止。有些业余兴趣明显更适合男生，有些更适合女生，但在学校里男生和女生选择的差异很小，如果把男女生进行的活动分开的话，只会造成不

and girls from an early age until, at the end of their school life, they go on to the university or to their business or professional training. A few of the pursuits to be mentioned are obviously more appropriate for boys, others for girls; but the differences between those that are followed in schools for boys and those for girls are surprisingly small, and to give separate lists would only involve much needless repetition.

For the sake of clearness, it may be well to group the various activities according as they are mainly outdoor or indoor occupations. In the outdoor group, games and sports need not be included, as being, in most cases, as much a part of the ordinary school course as the class-work. They only become free-time pursuits, in the sense here intended, in so far as practice for them is optional, and a large amount of free time spent upon it. Thus, for example, while swimming is, or should be, compulsory for all, and a regular time found for it in the school time-table, it is entirely a voluntary matter to go in, as in many schools a large number do, for the tests of the Royal Humane Society. Apart from games, the outdoor pursuit that occupies the largest place is probably, in most of these schools, some branch of natural history（which may perhaps be held to include geology as well as the study of plant and animal life）—not so much by the making of collections, though this usually serves as a beginning, as by the keeping of diaries, notes of observations illustrated by drawings and photographs, and experimental work, in connection, perhaps, with work done in science classes. Similarly in the study of archaeology, visits to places of interest—there are always many old churches within reach, if not other buildings of equal interest—give matter for written notes as well as for drawings and photographs; and in at least one case, the fact that the neighbourhood is rich in Roman remains has given opportunity, under the guidance of a keen classical archaeologist, for the laying bare of more than one Roman villa, and for making interesting additions to the school museum. Besides their use in the service of other pursuits, sketching and photography also have many votaries for their own sake, though the former is usually more dependent on encouragement from above. Then there is gardening. The tenure of a plot of ground is a joy to many children; and in the opinion of the writer, some experience, and some experimental work, in the growing of the most necessary food plants, as

必要的重复。

　　为了把这个问题说得更清楚，我们可以把不同种类的活动分成户外活动和室内活动。就户外活动而言，游戏比赛和体育活动就不包括在内了，因为大部分情况下，这些活动已经和课堂学习一样成为学校日常课程的一部分。只有当学生有选择性地进行这些活动，并把大量自由时间花在上面，它们才能成为业余消遣。例如，如果游泳是所有学生的必修课（当然也应该是），学校的时间表上会有固定的时间分配，那么很多学校的很多学生就会自愿参加英国溺水者营救会的考试。除了体育比赛，在大多数这种学校里，最重要的户外活动可能和自然历史的某些分支有关（可能也包括地理和动植物的研究），不一定是标本制作——虽然这是学习自然历史的起步工作，有可能是通过写日记，做配有插图和照片的观察报告，或做实验来等，和理科课堂中的学习联系起来。同样，在考古研究中，参观古迹（如果没有其他同样令人感兴趣的建筑的话，总有很多古老的教堂可以参观）是写报告、绘图和照相的绝佳素材。而且，如果某个地方保留了很多古罗马遗迹，至少有机会由一个热心的考古学家指导，把某些古罗马建筑搞清楚，为学校博物馆增加些有趣的信息。素描和摄影本身也有很多爱好者，不过因为可以为其他活动服务，的确有不少人为了上述原因而学习素描和摄影。接下来是园艺。有一小块地，对很多孩子而言是一种乐趣。有些作家认为，不论是在课堂，还是在课余时间，种植某些常见的蔬菜或花卉，应该成为每一个人在某个阶段教育中的一部分。对有些人而言，如果条件允许的话，甚至可以种果树，养蜜蜂、家禽，做农活，等等。战时的需要让有些活动进入了学校，这的确对教育有益，不

well as flowers, should form part of the education of all at a certain stage, whether in school time or in free time. For some, where the conditions are favourable, this can be extended to the care of fruit-trees, bees, poultry, and to some kinds of farm-work. The needs of war-time have brought something of this into many schools, to the real gain of education, now and later, if it can be retained, at least as a possibility of choice. So also with the care of the playing fields: the more that the work needed for a game is thrown upon the players themselves, the more does it contribute to education. And so too with constructive work of any kind that, with some help of suggestion or direction, is within the compass even of comparatively unskilled labour. A lengthy list could be given of things accomplished in this way, with an educational value all the greater for their practical purpose, from Ruskin's [1] famous road down to the last field levelled and pavilion built or shed put up, by voluntary effort and in time found by the workers without encroaching on regular school work. And lastly, an outdoor occupation for free time which, in the earlier days of school life, we shall do well to encourage—both for its own value and the manifold interests that it encourages and lessons that it teaches, and also for its bearing on questions of national service that will remain to be answered after the war—is the wide range of activities comprised in scouting, undoubtedly one of the chief educational advances of our time. Whatever differences of views there may be on the wider questions of military service for national defence, and of making military training a specific part of education, few can deny that, with a view to national service of *some* kind, the use made by Sir Robert Baden-Powell of instincts natural to all at a particular stage of growth, by an organisation which can be kept entirely free from the failings of militarism, is a development of the utmost educational, as well as national, value. If a school already develops, by other means, all the activities trained by scouting, and utilises in other ways the instincts and motives to which it makes appeal, there may be little or nothing to be gained by its adoption. But of how many schools can this be said? For the rest it undoubtedly

---

① Ruskin：此处可能指 John Rustkin（约翰·罗斯金，1819~1900），19 世纪英国杰出的作家和美术评论家、社会活动家，在建筑领域也卓有建树。他对社会的评论使他被视为道德领路人或预言家。其著作《留给这个后来者》（*Unto This Last*）曾对甘地产生过影响。他于 1870~1879 年和 1883~1884 年两次担任牛津大学的美术教授。

管是现在还是以后，这至少应该作为一个选择保留下来。在操场上进行的活动也一样：一项运动对一个运动员要求得越多，对教育越有帮助。所有建设性的工作也是如此，有专业人士的建议和指导的话，这些工作可以纳入非技术性劳动的范围。这样的例子可以列出一长串，这些活动因为实用性而更具教育意义。从罗斯金的著名道路到平整的田野，从新建的亭子到搭起的棚子，都是由学生自己努力，并且在没有影响正常学业的情况下完成的。最后，我们应当积极鼓励的，是一项应该在学校生活中尽早开展的业余户外活动——童子军的各项活动；不论是为了活动本身的价值，还是为了它们可以鼓励的兴趣、可能给学生的教训，或者为了鼓励学生积极为国服务（这当然要等到战后才能看出来），童子军活动都是我们这个时代最有教育价值的活动。对于为了国防目的而服兵役，对于把军训作为教育的一个具体部分，不论有多少不同意见，都没有人能否认其价值。正如罗伯特爵士所说，在每一个人成长的某个阶段，都会出于本性想为国效力。不论是哪一种活动，如果能把这种天性组织起来，既可以避免其服务于军国主义，又有最大的教育意义和民族意义。相反，如果一所学校通过其他方法，发展了童子军的所有活动，用其他方式利用了这些本能和动机，那些活动的意义就不大了。但有多少学校是这样做的呢？如果大家承认上述做法是有道理的话，那么对其他学校而言，童子军的活动由于在学生成长过程中的适当阶段提供了一种个人发展的途径，因而在现在显得尤其重要。除此之外，如果童子军的活动还能解决为国服兵役的问题，免除大规模征兵的需要，那么我们完全有理由明确其重要位置，鼓励其在学校进行所有适当的活动。

offers a way of doing, at the stage of growth for which it is best fitted, much of what, if there is any truth in what has been urged above, is, from the point of view of individual development, of greater importance now than ever before. If, in addition to this, it will go far to solve the problem of national service, and to remove the need for conscription in the continental form, there is every reason to give it a prominent place in the activities encouraged, if not insisted upon, at school.

Let us now turn to the group of indoor pursuits, which, if they have not quite so direct a bearing upon health, are in another way even more important; for a large part of leisure, even at school and still more, in all probability, afterwards, falls at times and under conditions that make some indoor occupation necessary, and the waste or misuse of these times is likely to be greater. In this group certain things need be no more than mentioned, as either applying, at any given time, only to a few picked individuals, or else likely, in the majority of schools, to be made a regular part of the school routine; such as, of the one kind, the editing of the school magazine, or membership of the school fire-brigade with the frequent practices that this involves; or, of the other kind, special gymnastics（including such things as boxing and fencing）, or lectures and concerts and other entertainments given to the school, as distinguished from those given by members of it, the preparation for which gives occupation beforehand to much of their leisure. Of the free-time pursuits more properly so called, in which many can share, the commonest are probably the various school societies. Most schools have one or more debating societies, with meetings at regular intervals throughout the winter terms, for the discussion of questions of general or special interest; the difficulty being more often to find a subject than speakers. Many also have Essay or Literary societies, for reading papers and discussing the books and writers treated of, which involve a considerable amount of previous reading. Besides these most schools now have similar societies, in addition to those for carrying out the field-work already mentioned, for holding lectures and discussions on various branches of science. Some also have a musical society for gaining fuller acquaintance with the works of the chief composers; and a dramatic society for reading and acting plays as occasion allows. Allied with these interests is voluntary laboratory work in some branch of science, both by individuals

下面我们谈谈室内活动，这些活动即使对健康没有太直接的影响，从其他方面来看也更为重要。因为无论是在校的时候，还是毕业以后，大部分闲暇时光都更有利于从事室内活动，这些时间，如果浪费或者误用的话，也更为可惜。这一类活动有些在任何情况下，都只适用于少数选拔出来的人，或者，在大多数学校，是作为学校常规活动的一部分。例如，一类是校刊编辑活动、实践性很强的学校消防，另一类是特殊体育项目（比如拳击和击剑）、校内讲座、音乐会和其他娱乐活动。和专业人士组织不同的是，这些活动都需要提前用很多业余时间准备。在业余活动中，大多数人都可以加入的、最普遍的就是各种学校社团。大部分学校都有一个或几个辩论组织，在冬季学期定期开会，讨论或大众或特殊的问题。辩手好找，而好的辩题却不太好找。很多学校还有散文社或文学社，其目的是读书和讨论规定的书和作者，这需要预先做很多准备工作。很多学校还有其他类似的社团，除了上面提及的开展田野调查的团体、就科学的各个分支举办讲座和讨论的社团，有些学校还有音乐方面的社团，帮助成员了解主要作曲家的作品；有戏剧社团，成员阅读戏剧作品，有机会的时候表演作品。和这些兴趣密切相关的是某些领域的实验，有些是个人单独进行，有些是集体进行。这些实验完全可以被视为一种研究，即使他们可能只是重新去发现前人已经发现的成果。有些学校会提供专门经费，鼓励天文方面的这类实验，有些学校鼓励无线电研究，或者蔬菜染色剂的使用，等等。这些工作，年龄小一些的学生都可以参与，这就为个人创新开拓了广阔的领域。

除了这些智力方面的兴趣，还有更广泛的爱好，各

and groups, which may not unfairly be dignified with the name of research, even if it is only the re-discovery of what has been worked out by others. In some schools special provision is made for encouraging optional work of this kind in astronomy; in others it may be wireless telegraphy, or the use of vegetable dyes, and so forth. In some of this work even the younger can take part; and of the many reasons for its encouragement not the least is the wide field it opens to individual initiative.

Besides all these more specially intellectual interests, and of still wider appeal, various kinds of handicrafts afford abundant occupation, some for the longer and some also for the shorter periods of leisure. Wood-work, carving, work in metal or leather, pottery, basket-plaiting, bookbinding, needlework and embroidery, knitting, netting hammocks and so forth—the only limit to the number of such crafts is the limit to the knowledge and energy of those who can start and direct them, and to the space available, as some can only be carried on in rooms reserved for such work. So, too, with various kinds of art-work—drawing, modelling, lettering, making posters for entertainments; or music, both individual and concerted, orchestra practice, part-singing, glee-clubs and so on; or morrice and other folk-dances, now happily being widely revived. And lastly there are indoor games, some of which, like chess（cards are probably best confined to the sanatorium）, have a high training value, and others afford a useful occasional outlet to high spirits; and entertainments got up by some society, or perhaps by a single form, for the rest of the "house" or school, such as a concert or play or even an occasional fancy-dress dance, the preparation for which will happily occupy free time for as long beforehand as is allowed, and does much to encourage ingenuity, especially if strict conditions are imposed that all that is required must be made for the purpose and not bought.

But by this time many questions will have arisen in the mind of the reader, especially if much of what has been enumerated lies outside his school experience; questions that demand an immediate answer. Even if all this free-time work and play may have a certain value, how can time be found for it without encroaching on the regular work and games which, after all, must be the main concern of the school? And even supposing that time could be found for both, will not all this voluntary activity and pleasure-work absorb the interests and energies that ought to be given to the more

种手工活动能提供很多长期或者短期的消遣。木工、雕刻、金属或皮革工艺、陶艺、编织、书籍装订、针线和刺绣、针织、织网，等等，这些活动在参加人数上没有限制，唯一限制就是指导人员的知识和精力，还有就是活动场所，因为有些只能在专门的地方进行。同样，各种个人或者集体的艺术活动，比如管弦乐队、合唱团、男声俱乐部等的活动，以及莫里斯和其他民间舞，现在都很盛行。最后，还有各种室内活动，有些，比如棋类（打扑克最好只限于疗养所）有很高的训练价值，而其他活动则能很好地放松紧张情绪。为某机构某学校举行的社团活动或一次性的活动，例如音乐会、戏剧表演或者化装舞会，其准备工作都需要较长的时间，也能极大地激发独创精神，特别是如果严格规定所有用具都必须自己制作而不能花钱购买的话。

读到这儿，读者心中可能会有很多问题，想要立刻得到解答，特别是如果上述很多东西超出其经验的话。即使所有这些业余爱好都有一定价值，如何为他们安排足够的时间，同时又不占用正规学习和体育活动的时间？毕竟，这些才是学校的主要任务。而且，假设可以为两者都保证足够的时间，这些自愿活动和娱乐难道不会分散本来应该放在更严肃（当然不是那么吸引人）的学习上的兴趣和精力吗？还有，如何合理控制这么广泛的活动？谁来教授或者管理这些活动？如何维持这些活动的运转？这些活动应该是必修的，还是学生可选可不选？还是可以像花蝴蝶一样，东做做，西做做，结果一无所获，浪费精力？

对于这些问题我只能尝试给出一个简要的答案。这个答案就暗含在人们对自古以来一种难题的解答方法之中：solvitur ambulando（It is solved by walking，在行进中解决）。因为，如果有了清晰的目

serious, if less attractive, studies? And again, how can all this wide range of activity be controlled? Who is going to teach, or look after, all these things? How are they to be kept going? Are they, or any of them, to be compulsory, or is a boy or girl to be allowed to do anything or nothing, or to flit, butterfly-fashion, from one to another, learning nothing except to fritter away energy in endless mental dissipation?

Only a brief answer can be attempted to these questions. It might indeed be given in the answer to the old puzzle, *solvitur ambulando*; for, given a clear aim and common sense, most difficulties in education disappear as one goes on. It is, in fact, a question of educational values; that settled, matters of detail soon settle themselves. From what has been said above, it will be plain that the writer is one of those who think these voluntary free-time activities of such value that they are willing, in order to make room for them, to jettison some of the traditions that have gathered about school work and games. Let the morning hours be reserved for the severer kinds of class work, but let the afternoons be mainly given to active pursuits of other kinds as well as games; and on one of them at least let expeditions in pursuit of the outdoor interests above outlined be an alternative to the games chosen by the keen players, or compulsory for those without an equivalent hobby. Then, too, in the evenings let preparation be varied with handicrafts（the result will be an intellectual gain rather than loss）, and time be reserved for the meetings of societies or for entertainments. It may be well to say here that while every one of the things above mentioned is an actual fact in some school, in none, probably, are all attempted at once, nor, of course, do any of their members take up many of these pursuits at the same time; but it is surprising how much can be done by treating a part of some afternoons and evenings in the week as leisure time for these pursuits. When this is done, there is usually a particular member of the Staff whose task it is, either permanently or in rotation, to see what is being done, to give suggestions and encouragement to beginners, and to see, if necessary, that freedom does not mean disorder. Naturally, in the case of handicrafts, others also take part as actual teachers or at least as fellow-workers; but though it is generally helpful for members of the Staff to join in all such work and in discussions, the aim of it all is likely to be more fully attained if as much as possible of the organisation and direction

的和常识，教育中的大多数难题都会在一个人前进的
道路上迎刃而解。这实际上是教育的价值问题；这个
问题解决了，细节问题就自然而然解决了。从上面讨
论中可以看出，作者认为这些自愿的业余活动就属于
这类问题，为了给这些活动一点空间，可以放弃学习
和体育比赛上的某些传统。上午的时间应该留给严肃的
课堂学习，但下午可以主要用来积极进行其他活动和体
育比赛，这些活动中至少要有一种具有冒险精神的户外
活动，可以让狂热的体育分子在比赛之外还有一个选
择，或者也可以规定没有同类爱好的人必须选择一项。
然后，晚上可以进行各种手工活动（结果肯定会对智
力发展有益），还可以留一些给社团活动和娱乐。可
以大胆地说，虽然有些学校安排了上面提到的每一种
活动，但是没有一项活动可以吸引所有人，同样，也
不可能有人可以同时尝试多种活动。但如果把每周下
午和晚上的有些固定时间安排给这些业余活动，其结
果肯定会令人惊讶。这样的话，教师中必须安排一个
人员，不论是固定人员还是大家轮流，来检查活动的
完成情况，来给初学者提供建议和鼓励，来保证自由
时间不是一片混乱。虽然在手工活动中，如果教师来
参加所有活动和讨论、学校工作人员来组织和指导的
话，会更有帮助，会更好地实现活动的目的。其实，
其他人也可以作为指导老师或者至少是合作成员。必
修的问题也一样，并非每一个人都很清楚地了解他想
做什么，有时候兴趣仅仅来自实践。因此，必须认识
到，在某些阶段，每一个人都必须选择一种爱好，当
然个人选择的自由度越大，选择的范围越广，结果越好。
不是所有的乡间散步都必须有个目的地，不是所有积极
利用的时间都应该拿来读书，但如果没有一个具体目标，
很少有人能养成散步的习惯，进而学会了解和热爱乡

is left to members of the school. So, too, with the question of compulsion. Not all have so strong a bent as to know what they want to do, and sometimes interests come only by actual experience. It is well, therefore, to have an understanding that, at certain times, all must follow some one of the possible occupations; but the more it can be left to the individual choice, and the wider the range of choice, the better for the purpose we have in view. Not all country rambles need have a definite object, nor all time be actively filled that might be left for reading. But without a definite object few will make a habit of walking, or learn to know and love the country; and not all, especially where there is a multiplicity of other interests, will form the habit of reading unless regular times are set apart for it, times when books must be read and not merely magazines. How far freedom of change from one occupation to another is desirable is largely an individual question. The younger need to try many things before they can settle down to one, in order to discover their real interests and to exercise their faculties. But it is well to have a strict limit to the number of things that may be taken up at once, and a fixed length of time to be given to each before it may be replaced by another. With the older, this, as a rule, settles itself, on the one hand by growing interest in one or two directions, and on the other by the increasing demands of the school work and approaching examinations. It is the younger, therefore, who need most encouragement. In schools where, as said above, there is a long tradition of such free-time work, there is the less need for anything beyond suggestions and general supervision. Yet even in these it is found helpful to have, at the beginning of the year, talks upon the subject by some member of the Staff, or an old boy perhaps who has devoted himself to some particular branch, in order to explain what can be done and the standard to be maintained. In several of them prizes are offered every year, either by the school or by the Old Scholars' Association or by individual old scholars, for good work in many of the categories mentioned above; these in some schools being the only prizes given. In some cases they are money prizes, as in certain kinds of work the tools or materials used are costly; in others the prizes are not given to individuals, but in the form of a "trophy" to the form or "house" that shows up the best record for the term or year; in others, again, the need of prizes is not felt, but interest and keenness to maintain a

村；同样，如果不规定一个固定时间读书而不仅仅是读
杂志，也不是所有人都能养成阅读的习惯，特别是生活
中还有很多其他兴趣可供选择的时候。至于可以在多大
程度上自由地从一种兴趣转移到另一种兴趣，那就是个
人的问题了。年轻一些的人在确定某种兴趣之前可以多
做尝试，以便发现他们真正的兴趣所在，锻炼他们的能
力。但最好对同时尝试的种类有一个严格的限制，每种
兴趣在被另外一种代替之前有一段固定尝试时间。对
年纪大一些的人来说，则需要一边发展一到两个方面
的兴趣，一边准备应对日益加重的学业和越来越近的
考试。因此，年轻一些的学生更需要鼓励。在上面提
及的具有长期业余活动传统的学校，仅需要提点建议
和一般监管就足够。即使在这样的学校，最好在学年
的开始，由教师或者精通某个特殊活动的学长来介绍
这项活动，来解释哪些是可以做的，要遵守的标准是
什么。有些活动，每年还会颁奖给表现优异的成员，
颁奖典礼可能由学校主持，也可能是学者联合会或者
某一个老资格的学者主持。这甚至可能是有些学校唯
一的颁奖活动。有时候，奖励可能是奖金，因为有些
活动的工具和材料很贵；有些情况下，奖励可能不是
颁发给个人，而且以奖杯的形式颁给学期或者学年最
佳纪录团队；有些活动没有奖励，但每年会举办一
次公共展出或表演来展示其所取得的成就，从而保
持大家对这些活动的兴趣和热情。还有些活动最大
的刺激就是，它们本身就是某些研究的分支，从中
可以获得更大的自由，比如徒步或者骑单车到某些地
方探险。

　　当然，有这么多活动，可能也会有一种风险，就是
学生的大部分精力被这些活动吸引走了，留给日常学习
的就很少了。在少数情况下，有些学生有很好的天赋，

good standard are kept up by the public show, held each year, of work done in leisure time. And, it may be added, a great stimulus in itself is the wider freedom that can be earned by those who follow certain branches of study, in the way, for instance, of expeditions, on foot or by bicycle, to places where they can be pursued.

But with all this there is, of course, the danger that so much energy may be absorbed in these pursuits that little is left for the ordinary school work. In some few cases, where there is a strong natural bent and the free-time pursuit is a serious object of study, this may be a thing not to be discouraged, as it will provide the truest means of education. But in most cases care is needed to see that the due proportion is kept, and especially that mere amusement is not allowed to occupy the whole of leisure, still less to distract thought and effort from serious work. By making entertainments, which might, if too frequent or too elaborate, have this effect, dependent on the school work being well done, this danger can be minimised. For the rest, if free-time work is found to take the first place in a boy's thoughts, may not this be a sign that the ordinary curriculum and methods of teaching are capable of improvement, and that more use of these natural interests may with advantage be made in class time as well? Not that work of any kind can be all pleasure or always outwardly interesting; there is plenty of hard spade-work needed in any study seriously followed, in class or out. But if in education keenness is the first essential and personality the final aim, interest and freedom must have a larger place than is usually allowed them in the class-room if the real education is not to centre in the self-chosen and self-directed pursuits of leisure.

One word more. It must not be supposed that all that has been described is only possible, or only needed, in the boarding school or only for a specially leisured class. If, as has here been urged, these activities and interests form an integral part of education in its fullest meaning, they are just as necessary in the day school and cannot be left to chance and the home to see to. And of all the needed reforms in elementary education, amongst the most needed is the greater utilisation of the active interests and instincts of children, in a training that would have a wider outlook and a closer bearing, through practical experience, both on the work of life and the use of leisure.

业余活动又正好是学习的一部分，这种情况当然应该鼓励，因为它提供了一种真正的教育。但是，大多数情况下，学生必须合理分配业余活动和学习的时间，尤其是纯粹的娱乐活动绝对不能占据所有业余时间，不能分散学生在学习上的心思和努力。娱乐活动太频繁、太费神的话，的确会造成这种后果，但如果要求学生先好好完成学习任务的话，这种危险就可以尽量消除了。在其他情况下，如果业余爱好成了一个学生心中最重要的东西，难道不能说明日常教学安排和教学方法需要改进吗？难道不能说明更好地利用学生天生的兴趣也许会对课堂教学更有帮助吗？当然，不是所有的学习和活动都从头到尾让人愉快，或者总是一下子就让人感兴趣的。很多工作非常困难，无论是课内还是课外都需要付出很多努力。但如果在教育中，兴趣是第一要素，性格是最终目的，如果真正的教育不是以自我选择和自我主导的业余追求为中心的话，兴趣和自由应该在课堂中占据更重要的地位。

再多说一点，这儿谈到的所有活动，并非只有在寄宿学校和特别有空闲时间的班级才可能或者有必要进行。这些活动和兴趣在日校也很必要，不是可有可无或只在家里进行，它们应该成为教育中不可分割的一部分，并发挥其全部作用。在小学教育改革中，最需要的就是对孩子们天性和兴趣的更好利用，通过在生活和利用闲暇方面的实际经验，培养学生更广阔的视野和更集中的能力。

在很多职业中，一开始需要的不是技术知识，而是训练有素的头脑。

——J.D.马克克雷爵士

PREPARATION FOR PRACTICAL LIFE

By SIR J. D. McCLURE
Head Master of Mill Hill School [1]

It is, perhaps, the chief glory of the Ideal Commonwealth that each and every member thereof is found in his right place. His profession is also his vocation; in it is his pride; through it he attains to the *joie de vivre* [2] ; by it he makes his contribution to the happiness of his fellows and to the welfare and progress of the State. The contemplation of the Ideal, however, would seem to be nature's anodyne for experience of the Actual. In practical life, all attempts, however earnest and continuous, to realise this ideal are frustrated by one or more of many difficulties; and though the Millennium follows hard upon Armageddon, we cannot assume that in the period vaguely known as "after the war" these difficulties will be fewer in number or less in magnitude. Some of the more obvious may be briefly considered.

In theory, every child is "good for something"; in practice, all efforts to discover for what some children are good prove unavailing. The napkin may be shaken never so vigorously, but the talent remains hidden. In every school there are many honest fellows who seem to have no decided bent in any direction, and who would probably do equally well, or equally badly, in any one of half-a-dozen different employments. Some of these boys are steady, reliable, not unduly averse from labour, willing—even

---

①   Mill Hill School: 米尔希尔学校，英国著名私立中学，创办于 1807 年，位于伦敦市郊，原为男校，20 世纪末期才改为男女校。学校的教学宗旨是为学生提供广泛的教育，让他们在学业、文化、体育及社交方面有所发展，成为有领导才能及有责任感的人。

②   Jioe de vivie: 法语，意为生活的乐趣。

论实际生活之准备

J. D. 马克克雷爵士
米尔希尔学校校长

如果每一个社会成员都能在社会中找到其恰当的位置，这可能是一个理想社会最大的荣耀。在这样一个社会中，一个人的职业同时也是他的兴趣、他的骄傲，他从中可以获得生活的乐趣，同时为民众的幸福和社会的福祉进步做出自己的贡献。对理想国的沉思，好像是自然所赋予人们对实际生活经历的止痛剂。在实际生活中，所有的努力，无论发自内心、持之以恒的程度如何，都会因为这样或那样的困难而偃旗息鼓。在第一次世界大战后的这个新千年里，世事艰难，我们想必不能确定，战后时期，这些困难在数量上会减少，在程度上会降低。事实上，有些困难甚至会更为明显。

从理论上说，每个孩子都"擅长某样东西"，但在实践中，要发现他们擅长什么非常困难。我们比以往任何时候都努力开掘，但孩子们的天赋还是没有显露。在每个学校都有很多诚实的学生，他们好像没有任何明确的偏好，在几种工作中可以做得同样好，或者同样糟糕。这些学生有的很稳重、很可靠，喜欢劳动，愿意甚至渴望接受指导，但没有在任何一种工作上显示出天赋和

anxious—to be guided and to carry out instructions, yet are quite unable to manifest a preference for any one kind of work.

Others, again, show real enthusiasm for a business or profession, but do not possess those qualities which are essential to success therein; yet they are allowed to follow their supposed bent, and spend the priceless years of adolescence in the achievement of costly failure. Many a promising mechanic has been spoiled by the ill-considered attempts to make a passable engineer; and the annals of every profession abound in parallel instances of misdirected zeal. In saying this, however, one would not wish to undervalue enthusiasm, nor to deny that it sometimes reveals or develops latent and unsuspected talents.

The life-work of many is determined largely, if not entirely, by what may be termed family considerations. There is room for a boy in the business of his father or some other relative. The fitness of the boy for the particular employment is not, as a rule, seriously considered; it is held, perhaps, to be sufficiently proved by the fact that he is his father's son. He is more likely to be called upon to recognise the special dispensations of a beneficent Providence on his behalf. It is natural that a man should wish the fruits of his labour to benefit his family in the first instance, at any rate; and the desire to set his children well on the road of life's journey seems entirely laudable. It is easy to hold what others have won, to build on foundations which others have laid, and to do this with all their experience and goodwill to aid him. Hence when the father retires he has the solid satisfaction of knowing that

Resigned unto the Heavenly Will,

His son keeps on the business still.

It cannot be denied that this policy is often successful; but it is equally undeniable that it is directly responsible for the presence of many incompetent men in positions which none but the most competent should occupy. There are many long-established firms hastening to decay because even they are not strong enough to withstand the disastrous consequences of successive infusions of new (and young) blood.

Many, too, are deterred from undertaking congenial work by reason of the inadequate income to be derived therefrom, and the unsatisfactory prospects which it presents. Let it suffice to mention the teaching profession, which fails to attract in

倾向。

另外有些学生，对某项事业非常热情，但却不具备成功所需的基本素质，即使让他们发展某项看起来好像具有的才能，并允许他们把青年时期宝贵的岁月花在发展这种才能上，最终他们却难以获得成功。很多大有前途的机械师，却被误导去当工程师。每一种职业都可以列出大量被误导的例子。说到这些，我们不是要低估热情的重要性，也不是要否认热情有时候会展示或发展隐藏的天赋和潜能。

很多人的终身职业，在很大程度上甚至是完全由家庭因素决定的。一个人很可能从事父亲或者亲友从事的职业。至于他是否适合这个工作，通常没有人严肃思考过，而早已充分证明的事实是他是他父亲的儿子。他必须从自身的角度充分认识到对他有益的天意。自然，一个人首先会希望他的劳动果实能使家庭受益，不论从任何角度来说，他希望自己的子女能在人生的道路上一帆风顺，也是完全可以理解和值得赞许的。在其他人成功的基础上继续，利用他们的经验和善意是一件很容易的事情。因此，一个父亲退休后，最满意的是发现：

听从天意，

子承父业。

无可否认，这项策略常常很成功，但同样不可否认的是，这直接导致了现在很多才能不够的人，占据了最具才华的人才能胜任的位置。很多历史悠久的公司很快毁灭仅仅是因为无法承受源源不断的新鲜血液注入所带来的灾难性的后果。

很多人没有从事喜欢的工作，是因为收入太低或者

any considerable numbers the right kind of men and women. A large proportion of its members did not become teachers from deliberate choice, but, having failed in their attempt to secure other employment, were forced to betake themselves to the ever-open portals of the great Refuge for the Destitute, and become teachers（or, at least, become classified as such）. True there are a few "prizes" in the profession, and to some of the *rude donati* the Church holds out a helping hand; but the lay members cannot look forward even to the "congenial gloom of a Colonial Bishopric." ^①

Others, again, are attracted to employments（for which they may have no special aptitude）by the large salaries or profits which are to be earned therein, often with but little trouble or previous training—or so, at least, they believe. The idea of vocation is quite obscured, and a man's occupation is in effect the shortest distance from poverty which he cannot endure, to wealth and leisure which he may not know how to use. It frequently happens, too, that a young man is unable to afford either the time or the expense necessary to qualify for the profession which he desires to enter, and for which he is well adapted by his talents and temperament. Not a few prefer in such circumstances to "play for safety," and secure a post in the Civil Service.

It is plain from such considerations as these that all attempts to realise the Utopian ideal must needs be, for the present at least, but very partially successful. Politics are not the only sphere in which "action is one long second-best." Even if it were possible at the present time to train each youth for that calling which his own gifts and temperament, or the reasoned judgment of his parents, selected as his life-work, it is very far from certain that he would ultimately find himself engaged therein. English institutions are largely based on the doctrine of individual liberty, and those statutes which establish or safeguard individual rights are not unjustly regarded as the "bulwarks of the Constitution." But the inalienable right of a father to choose a profession for his son, or of the son to choose one for himself, is often exercised without any real inquiry into the conditions of success in the profession selected. Hence the frequent complaints about the "overcrowding of the professions" either in

---

① congenial gloom of a Colonial Bishopric：前途黯淡的殖民地主教。此处指在英国的殖民地担任一个城市或教区的高级神职人员或者首领，通常被认为是一种流放，没有太大的前途。

前途不明。教师这个职业就很能说明问题，因为这个工作很难吸引足够的合适人才。很多教育专业的人不愿意做老师，但尝试其他职业又失败了，最后不得不重新回到这个避难所再从事这个职业，因为它的大门永远都是敞开的。事实上，教师这个职业的"奖励"很少，偶尔教堂可能会向他们伸出援助之手，提供一些选择机会，但一个外行连"前途黯淡的殖民地主教"这个职位也难以奢望。

其他人，被某些工作（他们对这些工作没有太多天赋）吸引，主要是因为高薪和福利，麻烦很少，或者他们自认为有相关经验。人们对于工作的理念还很模糊，一个人的职业事实上是远离他难以忍受的贫困的捷径，是获得财富和闲暇的捷径，虽说他可能还不知道怎么使用财富和闲暇。常常，一个年轻人即使找到了自己渴望同时又符合个人性情和才能的工作，也难以花费大量的时间和昂贵的费用来学会这种工作所需的技能。在这种情况下，更多人倾向于更"安全的选择"，在政府部门中找个位置。

这样的考虑也很平常，正如所有想要实现乌托邦式的理想的努力，在目前最多也就是获得部分成功。在包括政治在内的很多领域里，宗旨都是"行动第二"。即使现在有可能这样训练每一个年轻人，根据他的天赋和性情，或者父母的合理判断，来选择他的终身职业，也远远不能确定他最终一定会从事这项工作。英国学校在很大程度上是建立在个人自由的基础上的，那些建立和维护个人权利的规章制度已经被认为是"宪法的保障"。不过一个父亲为儿子选择职业的权利，或者说一个儿子自己选择的权利仍然不可剥夺，虽然

certain localities or in the country at large. The Bar affords a glaring example. "There be many which are bred unto the law, yet is the law not bread unto them." The number of recruits which any one branch of industry requires in a single year is not constant, and, in some cases, is subject to great fluctuations; yet there are few or no statistics available for the guidance of those who are specially concerned with that branch, or who are considering the desirability of entering it. The establishment of Employment Exchanges is a tacit admission of the need of such statistics, and— though less certainly—of the duty of the Government to provide them. Yet even if they were provided it seems beyond dispute that, in the absence of strong pressure or compulsion from the State, the choice of individuals would not always be in accordance with the national needs. The entry to certain professions—for instance that of medicine—is most properly safeguarded by regulations and restrictions imposed by bodies to which the State has delegated certain powers and duties. It may happen that in one of these professions the number of members is greatly in excess, or falls far short of the national requirements; yet neither State nor Professional Council has power to refuse admission to any duly qualified candidate, or to compel certain selected people to undergo the training necessary for qualification. It is quite conceivable, however, that circumstances might arise which would render such action not merely desirable but absolutely essential to the national well-being; indeed it is at least arguable that such circumstances have already arisen. The popular doctrine of the early Victorian era, that the welfare of the community could best be secured by allowing every man to seek his own interests in the way chosen by himself, has been greatly modified or wholly abandoned. So far are we from believing that national efficiency is to be attained by individual liberty that some are in real danger of regarding the two as essentially antagonistic. The nation, as a whole, supported the Legislature in the establishment of compulsory military service; it did so without enthusiasm and only because of the general conviction that such a policy was demanded by the magnitude of the issues at stake. Britons have always been ready, even eager, to give their lives for their country; but, even now, most of them prefer that the obligation to do so should be a moral, rather than a legal one. The doctrine

他很少真正考虑在这个职业上获得成功的条件。结果，无论是在某些地区还是在全国范围内，总是有很多关于"职业过于拥挤"的抱怨。法律界提供了一个很好的例子。"有很多人生在法律界，但靠法律却挣不够面包钱。"工业的任何一个分支每年所需要人数不同，有时候，可能变化还很大。但关注甚至想要选择这些分支的人几乎完全没有参考数据。建立职业介绍所正好可以提供这些数据，这也是政府职责之所在。不过即使有了这些数据，无可争议的是，没有国家的压力和规定，个人的选择肯定不会总是符合国家的需求。某些领域，比如医学领域，由于国家赋予了某些机构相当的权力和责任，想要进入这些领域，必须遵从某些规则和限制。有可能在这些领域中，人数大大超出或者远远不够国家的要求，但无论国家还是专业指导机构都没有权力拒绝合格的申请人，或者强迫某些人选的人进行必要的资格训练。不难发现，这些行为不但有益，对国家福利也是绝对必要的。事实上，这些行为已经开始。维多利亚时代早期流行的准则，即一个社会的福祉要想得到最好的保障，应当允许每个人用自己的方法寻求个人的兴趣，已经大大改变甚至完全被抛弃了。我们完全不相信在保障国家效率的情况下也可以有个人自由，有些人甚至认为这两者是完全矛盾的。国家，作为一个整体，支持立法机构规定的义务兵役制度，这样做当然不是因为热情，而仅仅是因为坚信，问题的严重程度需要这样的政策。英国人随时准备甚至渴望为祖国献出生命，但即使是现在，大部分人都宁愿这是一个道德义务，而非一个法律义务。个人自由的原则意味着国家尽量不干涉个人行为。因

of individual liberty implies the minimum of State interference. Hence there is no country in the world where so much has been left to individual initiative and voluntary effort as in England; and, though of late the number of Government officials has greatly increased, it still remains true that an enormous amount of important work, of a kind which is elsewhere done by salaried servants of the State, is in the hands of voluntary associations or of men who, though appointed or recognised by the State, receive no salary for their services. Nor can it be denied that the work has been, on the whole, well done. A traditional practice of such a kind cannot be (and ought not to be) abandoned at once or without careful consideration; yet the changed conditions of domestic and international politics render some modification necessary.

If the Legislature has protected the purchaser—in spite of the doctrine of "caveat emptor"—by enactments against adulteration of food, and has in addition, created machinery to enforce those enactments, are not we justified in asking that it shall also protect us against incompetence, especially in cases where the effects, though not so obvious, are even more harmful to the community than those which spring from impure food? The prevention of overcrowding in occupations would seem to be the business of the State quite as much as is the prevention of overcrowding in dwelling-houses and factories. The best interests of the nation demand that the entrance to the teaching profession—to take one example out of many—should be safeguarded at least as carefully as the entrance to medicine or law. The supreme importance of the functions exercised by teachers is far from being generally realised, even by teachers themselves; yet upon the effective realisation of that importance the future welfare of the nation largely depends. Doubtless most of us would prefer that the supply of teachers should be maintained by voluntary enlistment, and that their training should be undertaken, like that of medical students, by institutions which owe their origin to private or public beneficence rather than to the State; nevertheless, the obligation to secure adequate numbers of suitable candidates and to provide for their professional training rests ultimately on the State. The obligation has been partially recognised as far as elementary education is concerned, but it is by no means confined to that branch.

It is well to realise at this point that the efficient discharge of the duty thus imposed

此，世界上没有哪个国家像英国一样，个人有如此多的空间来发展自己的开创精神和个人意愿，虽然近来政府官员人数在增长，但仍然有大量的重要工作在英国是由志愿者团体完成的，或者是由国家任命和承认但不拿薪水的人员完成的，而在其他国家这些工作肯定是由国家公务员来完成的。而且，从整体上说这些工作完成得很好。这种传统不能也不应该轻率地马上放弃，但国内外政治形势的变化要求这种传统也要做出一些必要的改变。

如果立法机构通过反对假冒伪劣食品的法律来保护消费者，而不管"货物出门，概不退换"的规定，而且建立机构来保障这些法案的实施，那我们也完全有理由来要求政府保障我们免于某些危害。某些行为的危害表面上看可能不是那么明显，但却比伪劣食品对社会更有害。阻止过多的人涌入某种职业，就像阻止住房和厂房过于拥挤一样是国家的责任。要保障一个国家的最佳利益，对于教育职业的准入（仅仅举一个例子）应该像对医学和法律职业的要求一样仔细。大家还远远没有认识到教师职业的重要性，包括教师自己也没有；只有有效地认识到教师的重要性，才能更好地保障一个国家将来的福祉。的确，大部分人还是倾向于教师职业应该是个人自愿选择，对训练教师应该像训练医学生一样，由私人或者某些公益性的机构而非国家机构来进行。事实上，应该基本由国家为教师提供专业训练，并保障有足够的人员参加这些训练。就小学教育而言，国家已经部分认识到这种义务，但义务绝不应该只限于这个层次。

必须很好地认识到，有效地免除某些责任，必然意

will of necessity involve a much greater degree of compulsion on both teachers and pupils than has hitherto been employed. The terrible spectacle of the unutilised resources of humanity, which everywhere confronts us in the larger relations of our national life, has been responsible for certain tentatives which have either failed altogether to achieve their object, or have been but partially successful. Much has been heard of the educational ladder—incidentally it may be noted that the educational sieve is equally necessary, though not equally popular—and some attempts have been made to enable a boy or girl of parts to climb from the elementary school to the university without excessive difficulty. To supplement the glaring deficiencies of elementary education a few—ridiculously few—continuation schools have been established. That these and similar measures have failed of success is largely due to the fact that the State has been content to provide facilities, but has refrained from exercising that degree of compulsion which alone could ensure that they would be utilised by those for whose benefit they were created. "Such continuation schools as England possesses," says a German critic, "are without the indispensable condition of compulsion." The reforms recently outlined by the President of the Board of Education show that he, at any rate, admits the criticism to be well grounded. A system which compels a child to attend school until he is fourteen and then leaves him to his own resources can do little to create, and less to satisfy, a thirst for knowledge. During the most critical years of his life—fourteen to eighteen—he is left without guidance, without discipline, without ideals, often without even the desire of remembering or using the little he knows. He is led, as it were, to the threshold of the temple, but the fast-closed door forbids him to enter and behold the glories of the interior. Year by year there is an appalling waste of good human material; and thousands of those whom nature intended to be captains of industry are relegated, in consequence of undeveloped or imperfectly trained capacity, to the ranks, or become hewers of wood and drawers of water. Many drift with other groups of human wastage to the unemployed, thence to the unemployable, and so to the gutter and the grave. The poor we have always with us; but the wastrel—like the pauper— "is a work of art, the creation of wasteful sympathy and legislative inefficiency."

味着对教师和学生赋予更多的义务。在国民生活中比较宏观的层面上，我们对于人文资源利用极为不足，这导致某些实验完全不能实现其目的，或者仅仅取得部分成功。很多人谈到教育梯度的问题，偶尔也有人注意到教育筛选的必要性，虽说不是同样流行，但大家还是努力使有天赋的学生能比较容易地从小学上到大学。为了弥补小学教育的不足，我们建立了很少的一些继续教育学校。这些和类似措施之所以没有取得成功，主要是因为国家仅仅满足于提供设施，而没有规定参加这类教育的义务程度，如果加以规定的话，本身就能保证利益相关的人士来推行这个政策。一个德国批评家说："英国的继续教育学校缺乏必要的义务教育政策。"教育局主席最近谈到教育改革的时候表示，他从任何程度上都承认这个批评是很有道理的。目前的制度是孩子们上学上到14岁，然后就自己安排，这几乎完全不能激发更不能满足他们对知识的渴望。在他们一生最关键的时期——14岁到18岁，他们没有指导，没有纪律，没有理想，甚至常常没有记住他们所学的那丁点知识，也没有使用这丁点知识的渴望。他们被带到了知识殿堂的门口，但紧闭的大门禁止他们入内，他们没有机会体会知识殿堂的辉煌。年复一年，很多有良好资质的人才被浪费了，成千上万可能成为企业家的人由于训练不够和能力不足，成了伐木工人和拉丝工人。很多人和其他社会渣滓随波逐流，没有工作，无所事事地终其一生。穷人肯定会一直存在，但流浪者就像乞丐一样"是一件艺术产物，是过度同情和法律不足的产物"。

但是我们在提及"国家"的时候，必须谨慎，以免错误地认为国家是天命的实体，有天赐的权力和智慧。

We must be careful, however, in speaking of "the State" to avoid the error of supposing that it is a divinely appointed entity, endowed with power and wisdom from on high. It is, in short, the nation in miniature. Even if the Legislature were composed exclusively of the highest wisdom, the most enlightened patriotism in the country, its enactments must needs fall short of its own standards, and be but little in advance of those of the average of the nation. It must still acknowledge with Solon [①]. "These are not the best laws I could make, but they are the best which my nation is fitted to receive." We cannot blame the State without, in fact, condemning ourselves. The absence of any widespread enthusiasm for education, or appreciation of its possibilities; the claims of vested interests; the exigencies of Party Government; and, above all, the murderous tenacity of individual rights have proved well-nigh insuperable obstacles in the path of true educational reform. On the whole we have received as good laws as we have deserved. The changed conditions due to the war, and the changed temper of the nation afford a unique opportunity for wiser counsels, and—to some extent—guarantee that they shall receive careful and sympathetic consideration.

It may be objected, however, that in taking the teaching profession to exemplify the duty of the State to assume responsibility for both individual and community, we have chosen a case which is exceptional rather than typical; that many, perhaps most, of the other vocations may be safely left to themselves, or, at least left to develop along their own lines with the minimum of State interference. It cannot be denied that there is force in these objections. It should suffice, however, to remark that, if the duty of the State to secure the efficiency of its members in their several callings be admitted, the question of the extent to which, and the manner in which control is exercised is one of detail rather than of principle, and may therefore be settled by the common sense and practical experience of the parties chiefly concerned.

A much more difficult problem is sure to arise, sooner or later, in connection with the utilisation of efficients. Some few years ago the present Prime Minister called

---

① Solon: 梭伦（公元前 638 ~ 前 559 年），生于雅典，出身于没落的贵族。梭伦是古代雅典的政治家、立法者、诗人，是古希腊七贤之一。梭伦在公元前 594 年出任雅典城邦的第一任执政官，制定法律，进行改革，史称"梭伦改革"。他在诗歌方面也有成就，诗作主要是赞颂雅典城邦及法律的。他是古希腊最杰出的政治家之一，也是一位多才多艺的诗人。

简而言之，国家是民族的实体。即使法律被赋予了最高的智慧、最开明的爱国主义，要完全执行也有难度，因此法律只要比一般普通民众的认识超前一点点就合适了。正如梭伦所说："这不是我能制定出来的最好的法律，而是目前大家所能接受的最好的法律。"我们在谴责国家的时候，也必须批评我们自己。我们普遍对教育缺乏热情，难以赞同教育所带来的种种可能；对既得利益的占有、对个人权利不顾一切的坚持，以及党派政府的危机，都使得真正的教育改革有着不可逾越的障碍。整体而言，我们的法律比较适合我们。战争引起了形势的改变和民族性情的改变，为我们提供了一个独一无二的机会来采纳更明智的决策，并在某种程度上保障大家认真和宽容地考量这些政策。

但是，可能会有人反对用教育这个职业为例来说明国家的责任，并阐释个人和集体应承担的责任。我们选了一个不太典型的例子。很多也许是大部分其他职业可以安全地留给个人，或者至少由职业本身自由发展，而尽量不让国家干涉。无可否认，这些反对都有道理。但是我们也有足够的理由认为，如果要由国家来保障国民在某些职业上的效率，那么这种保障的程度和方式就是一个细节问题而非原则问题，完全可以通过执行团体的常识和实际经验来解决。

迟早，会出现一个更为困难的问题，那就是执行效率的问题。几年前，现任首相希望大家注意到培训富人的过程中所产生的权力浪费问题。他说，富人接受了金钱能买到的最好的教育，他们的身体和大脑得到训练以后，却"过着无所事事的生活"，这是对"一流物资的愚蠢的浪费"。他们没有为世界做出贡献，而

attention to the waste of power involved in the training of the rich. They receive, he said, the best that money can buy; their bodies and brains are disciplined; and then "they devote themselves to a life of idleness." It is "a stupid waste of first-class material." Instead of contributing to the work of the world, they "kill their time by tearing along roads at perilous speed, or do nothing at enormous expense." It has needed the bloodiest war in history to reveal the splendid heroism latent in young men of this class. Who can withhold from them gratitude, honour, nay even reverence? But the problem still remains how are the priceless qualities, which have been so freely devoted to the national welfare on the battlefield, to be utilised for the greater works of peace which await us? Are we to recognise the right to be idle as well as the right to work? Is there to be a kind of second Thellusson Act[①] , directed against accumulations of leisure? Or are we to attempt the discovery of some great principle of Conservation of Spiritual Energy, by the application of which these men may make a contribution worthy of themselves to the national life and character? Who can answer?

But though it is freely admitted on all hands that some check upon aggressive individualism is imperatively necessary, and that it is no longer possible to rely entirely upon voluntary organisations however useful, there are not a few of our countrymen who view with grave concern any increase in the power and authority of the State. They point out that such increase tends inevitably towards the despotism of an oligarchy, and that such a despotism, however benevolent in its inception, ruthlessly sacrifices individual interests and liberty to the real or supposed good of the State; that even where constitutional forms remain the spirit which animated them has departed; that officialism and bureaucracy with their attendant evils become supreme, and that the national character steadily deteriorates. They warn us that we may pay too high a price even for organisation and efficiency; and, though it is natural that we should admire certain qualities which we do not possess, we ought not to overlook the fact that those methods which have produced the most perfect national organisation in the history of the world are also responsible for orgies of brutality without parallel

---

① Thellusson Act：若努欣法案。若努欣为 18 世纪英国商人，有大笔个人资产，并希望个人资产能通过子孙不断积累下去。

是"要么以危险的速度在路上打发时间，要么大把花钱却什么也没有做"。只有历史上最血腥的战争，才能把这些年轻人潜在的伟大的英雄主义揭示出来。有谁能否认他们其实也有知恩图报、捍卫荣誉和尊严的品质？但问题是，虽然他们曾经在战场上为了国家福祉而贡献过这些无价的品质，但如何才能把这些品质用在更为伟大的和平事业上呢？难道我们必须承认，就像人民有工作的权利一样，人民也有闲散的权利？或者可以再规定第二个若努欣法案，来反对过度的闲散吗？或者说我们可以试着发明某种伟大的储存原理来储存精神能量，并通过利用这些能量，让这些人为人民生活和国民性格做出应有的贡献吗？谁能回答这些问题呢？

但是，大家都承认必须对攻击性的个人主义有所钳制，都承认无论志愿者组织多么有用，我们也不能完全依赖这些组织，因为不少国人都慎重地意识到了国家在权威和权力方面的进步。他们指出，这种进步不可避免地会导致专制的寡头政治，而且这种专制，无论其概念多么仁慈，都会无情地为了国家的好处而牺牲个人的利益和自由。即使宪法制度并不鼓励这一点，官僚主义以及随之而来的各种危害也会变得压倒一切，国民性格也会因此不断变坏。他们警告我们可能要为机构和效率付出极大的代价。虽然我们会很自然地崇拜自己所不具有的某些品质，但我们也不应该忽视这个事实，即那些建立了历史上最完美的国家机构的方式，同时也在文明国家制造了无与伦比的野蛮行径。这些警告肯定是必要的，但它们仅仅意味着一系列行动可能会导致的危险，而非不可避免的后果，

among civilised peoples. That such warnings are needful cannot be doubted; but may it not be urged that they indicate dangers incident to a course of action rather than the inevitable consequences thereof? In adapting ourselves to new conditions we must needs take risks. No British Government could stamp out voluntaryism even if it wished to do so; and none has yet manifested any such desire. The nation does not want that kind of national unity of which Germany is so proud, and which seems so admirably adapted to her needs; for the English character and genius rest upon a conception of freedom which renders such a unity foreign and even repulsive to its temper. Whatever be the changes which lie before us, the worship of the State is the one form of idolatry into which the British people are least likely to fall.

The recent adaptation of factories and workshops to the production of war material is only typical of what goes on year by year in peace time, though, of course, to a less degree and in less dramatic fashion. Not only are men constantly adapting themselves and their machinery to changed conditions of production, but they are applying the experience and skill gained in the pursuit of one occupation to the problems of another for which it has been exchanged. The comparative ease with which this is done is evidence of the widespread existence of that gift which our enemies call the power of "muddling through," but which has been termed—without wholly sacrificing truth to politeness—the "concurrent adaptability to environment." The British sailor as "handy man" has few equals and no superiors, and he is, in some sort, typical of the nation. The testimony of Thucydides[①] to Themistocles[②] might with equal

---

① Thucydides: 修昔底德，又译修西得底斯（约公元前460~前396年）。出身于雅典富有的显贵之家，自幼接受良好的教育，他在战争之初即而立之年开始搜集资料准备写一部战史，倾其毕生精力撰写《伯罗奔尼撒战争史》，直至生命的最后时刻。修昔底德的史学成就足以代表希腊古典史学的最高水平。他全面发展了人本史观，运用朴素唯物主义的方法论，综合地探讨历史因果关系，探索人事的规律，清楚地认识到经济因素在历史发展进程中的重要作用，创立了比较科学的治史原则，是西方史学史上第一位真正具有批判精神和求实态度的历史学家，被誉为"求真的人"。

② Themistocles: 地米斯托克利（约公元前524~约前460年），雅典政治家、统帅。贵族出身，从公元前493年起多次当选雅典执政官。公元前493~前492年修建比雷埃夫斯港。公元前490年参与指挥马拉松之战，击败波斯军。主张发展海军，控制海洋，铸造海上利剑。公元前483年说服公民大会用开采银矿的收入扩建海军，建造三层桨战船，建立一支拥有200艘战船的舰队，使雅典成为海上强国。公元前480年当选为将军。温泉关失守后，组织雅典居民撤退，并参与指挥希腊海军在萨拉米斯海战中战胜波斯舰队。约公元前471年被逐出雅典。死于波斯。

所以也并非一定要付诸实践？要适应新的情况，肯定会冒风险。即使想这样做，也没有一个英国政府能完全摒弃志愿者组织，而到目前为止还没有哪个政府表露出这种意愿。我们国家并不想要德国人极为自豪的那种民族统一性，这种统一性和他们的需求完全一致，而英国人的性格和天性取决于自由的概念，这就导致了统一性和我们的民族性情是相互排斥的。无论前方面临怎样的变化，国家崇拜是英国人最不可能陷入的一种盲目崇拜。

最近很多工厂和作坊都习惯于制造战争材料，这其实同和平时期年复一年的制造一样，只不过规模没那么大，范围没那么广而已。不仅仅是人们自己和机械制造会不断地适应新的生产形势，如果工作不同了，人们还会把在一种工作中获得的经验和技巧使用到另外一种工作中，这种做法相对简单，也证明了我们的敌人所说的"敷衍了事"的情况是广泛存在的。但我们在没有完全因为委婉而不顾真相的情况下把其叫作"适应环境"。"万金油"式的英国水手很难有其他人可以匹敌，从某种类型上来说，也代表了我们这个民族的性格。从修昔底德到地米斯托克利，他们因为对环境的适应能力而最终取得成功，这可以同样真实地用到今天很多英国人身上。这种适应能力在现在的战争中可以从一开始就使协约国免于失败，所以我们希望和相信这也可以让他们获得最后的胜利。但是如果这种能力让其所有者忽视准备工作或者看不起组织工作，它就变成了一个陷阱，因为不管付出多大的代价，这种能力都不可能完全有效地替代准备和组织工作。但同时，我们也应该认识到，任何一种想要严肃地削弱

or even greater truth be applied to many Englishmen today. As this power in the present war saved the Allies [①] from defeat at the outset, so we hope and believe it will carry them on to victory at the last. Yet it becomes a snare if it leads its possessor to neglect preparation or despise organisation, for neither of which can it ever be an entirely satisfactory substitute, albeit a very costly one. At the same time we should recognise that any system of training which seriously impairs this power tends to deprive us of one of the most valuable of our national assets. It follows that, for the majority at least, exclusive or excessive specialisation in training—vocational or otherwise—so far from being an advantage, is a positive drawback; for, as we have seen, a large proportion of our youth manifest no marked bent in any particular direction, and of those who do but a small proportion are capable of that hypertrophy which the highest specialisation demands.

It is important to remember that, though school life is a preparation for practical life, vocational education ought not to begin until a comparatively late stage in a boy's career, if indeed it begins at all while he remains at school. On this it would seem that all professional bodies are agreed; for the entrance examinations, which they have accepted or established are all framed to test a boy's general education and not his knowledge of the special subjects to which he will afterwards devote himself. The evils of premature specialisation are too well known to require even enumeration, and they are increased rather than diminished if that premature specialisation is vocational. The importance of technical training as the means whereby a man is enabled rightly to use the hours of work can hardly be exaggerated; but the value of his work, his worth to his fellows, and his rank in the scale of manhood depend, to at least an equal degree, upon the way in which he uses the hours of leisure. It is one of the greatest of the many functions of a good school to train its members to a wise use of leisure; and though this is not always achieved by direct means the result is none the less valuable. In every calling there must needs be much of what can only be to all save its most enthusiastic devotees—and, at times, even to them—dull routine and drudgery. A man cannot do his best, or be his best, unless he is able to overcome the paralysing

---

① Allies：第一次世界大战时的协约国，第二次世界大战时的同盟国，此处指协约国。

这种能力的训练体系，都可能会剥夺我们民族财富中最有价值的东西之一。至少对多数人来说，训练上的过度专业化——在职业或者其他方面——都远非一个优点，而是一个缺陷。因为正如我们所发现的一样，大部分年轻人没有在任何一个具体方向上显示明显的倾向，只有一小部分有天赋的人才能适应这种极为专业化的训练。

虽然学校生活是为实际生活做准备，职业训练也应该在学校生活的晚些时候再开始，记住这点很重要。看起来，所有职业机构也同意这一观点，因为它们接受和设立的资格考试几乎都是测试一个学生的一般水平，而不是他以后可能要从事的专业学科的知识。过早学习某个专业的害处众所周知，这儿就不提了，如果是为了职业而这样做，害处就更大。对一个人进行技术训练，让他能正确地利用工作时间，这极其重要。但是一个人工作的价值、对其他人的价值、他在人群中的地位，同样取决于他如何利用闲暇时光。一所好学校最伟大的作用之一，就是教会学生如何明智地利用闲暇时间；虽然这常常不能通过直接的方式达成，但还是一样重要。在每一个职业中，都会有很多日常琐事，可能最有奉献精神的人也会感到厌烦。一个人只有克服了这些负面影响，并保持心理和精神上的新鲜感和刺激感，或者说"他的内心必须天天更新"，才能全力以赴，做到最好。很多机构都在为此努力，但校园记忆、同学友谊、业余爱好对此最起作用。很多学生在离开学校的时候，都培养了一种兴趣爱好——文学、科学或实践爱好。这些爱好既有道德价值，也有经济价值。而且还不止这些。对"面包研究"的沉迷，

influences thus brought to bear upon him by securing mental and spiritual freshness and stimulus; in other words his "inward man must be renewed day by day." There are many agencies which may contribute to such a result; but school memories, school friendships, school "interests" take a foremost place among them. Many boys by the time they leave school have developed an interest or hobby—literary, scientific or practical; and the hobby has an ethical, as well as an economic value. Nor is this all. Excessive devotion to "Bread Studies," whether voluntary or compulsory, tends to make a man's vocation the prison of his soul. Professor Eucken[1] recently told his countrymen that the greater their perfection in work grew, the smaller grew their souls. Any rational interest, therefore, which helps a man to shake off his fetters, helps also to preserve his humanity and to keep him in touch with his fellows. Dr A.C. Benson tells of a distinguished Frenchman who remarked to him, "In France a boy goes to school or college, and perhaps does his best. But he does not get the sort of passion for the honour and prosperity of his school or college which you English seem to feel." It is this wondrous faculty of inspiring unselfish devotion which makes our schools the spiritual power-houses of the nation. This love for an abstraction, which even the dullest boys feel, is the beginning of much that makes English life sweet and pure. It is the same spirit which, in later years, moves men to do such splendid voluntary work for their church, their town, their country, and even in some cases leads them "to take the whole world for their parish."

However much we may strive to reach the beautiful Montessori[2] ideal, the fact remains that there must be some lessons, some duties, which the pupil heartily dislikes and would gladly avoid if he could; but they must be done promptly and satisfactorily, and, if not cheerfully, at least without audible murmuring. Eventually he may, and

---

[1] Eucken：此处可能是指 Rudolf Christoph Eucken（1846~1926），鲁道尔夫·欧肯，德国哲学家。主要作品有《大思想家的人生观》《人生的主义与价值》《人与世界——生命的哲学》等。1908 年因作品《精神生活漫笔》获诺贝尔文学奖。曾在欧美多所大学任教。

[2] Montessori：玛丽亚·蒙特梭利（Maria Montessori，1870~1952），意大利幼儿教育学家。主要教育理念为：尊重儿童，以儿童为中心，给予儿童自由的选择权，着重智慧和品格的养成，尊重儿童的成长规律，教师是一个引导者，注重日常生活教育及感官教育，注重本土文化及跨文化教学等。

不管是自愿的还是被迫的，都有可能让一个人的工作成为其精神的寄托。欧肯教授最近告诉他的国人，他们在工作上表现得越完美，他们的灵魂就会变得越狭隘。因此，任何合理的兴趣，都会帮助一个人摆脱枷锁，保持他的人性，保持他和其他人的联系。本森博士提及一个有名的法国人曾对他说："在法国，一个学生上学，可能会做到最好。但他不会像你们英国人一样，为学校的成功和荣誉感到与有荣焉。"正是这种激励无私奉献精神的非凡能力，使我们的学校成为民族的精神家园。这种对抽象事物的热爱，即使是最迟钝的学生都能感受到，并在很大程度上成为英国生活甜蜜而纯粹的开端。也正是这种精神，在往后的岁月中，推动英国人为他们的教堂、他们的城镇、他们的国家做出令人赞叹的志愿工作，甚至有时候"把全世界当作他们的教区"加以帮助。

无论我们多么努力去实现美丽的蒙特梭利式的教育理想，事实上学生总会从心底不喜欢一些课程、一些职责，如果可以的话，他们会很乐意逃避这些东西，但无论如何他们还是必须迅速而令人满意地完成这些任务，即使不太高兴，也不能抱怨出声。最后，他们也许会喜欢上这些东西，事实常常如此，他们会认识到这些并非是为了激怒或者惩罚他们，而是学校学习的一部分。学会做不喜欢的事——即使是被迫的，并把它养成一个习惯，对以后的生活是一个不错的准备，因为这是一个人的责任；因为每一个人，即使不喜欢，在很多时候都有不可避免、不可推卸和不可推迟的责任。

目前，一个真正的危险是：至少在有些地方，过于

often does, come to like them; at any rate he realises that they are not set before him in order to irritate or punish him, but as part of his school training. It will be agreed that the acquirement of a habit of doing distasteful things, even under compulsion, because they are part of one's duty is no bad preparation for a life in which most days bring their quota of unpleasant duties which cannot be avoided, delegated, or postponed.

At the present time, however, there is a real danger—in some quarters at least—of unduly emphasising the specifically vocational, or "practical" side of education. The man of affairs knows little or nothing of young minds and their limitations, of the conditions under which teaching is done, or of the educational values of the various studies in a school curriculum. He is prone to choose subjects chiefly or solely because of their immediate practical utility. Thus in his view the chief reason for learning a modern language is that business communications will thereby be facilitated. One could wish that he would be content to indicate the end which he has in view, and which he sees clearly, and leave the means of obtaining it to the judgment and experience of the teacher; for in education, as in other spheres of action, the obvious way is rarely the right way, and very often the way of disaster. Yet it is a distinct gain to have the practical man brought into the administration of educational affairs; for teachers are, as a rule, too little in contact with the world of commerce to know much of the needs and ideas of business men. The Board of Education has already established a Consultative Committee of Educationists. Why should not a similar standing Committee, consisting of representatives of the Chambers of Commerce of the country be also appointed? Such a Committee could render, as could no other body, invaluable service to the cause of education.

From a recent article by Professor Leacock [1] we learn that some twenty years ago there was a considerable change in the Canadian schools and universities. "The railroad magnate, the corporation manager, the promoter, the multiform director,

---

① Leacock: 此处可能是指 Stephen Butler Leacock（斯蒂芬·巴特勒·里柯克，1896~1944），加拿大著名学者和幽默作家、经济学家，也是加拿大第一位享有世界声誉的作家。在美国，他被认为是继马克·吐温之后最受欢迎的幽默作家。在加拿大有以他的名字命名的"里柯克幽默奖章"，从 1947 年开始颁给年度最佳幽默作家。

强调教育的职业或者实用功能。相关管理人士对年轻人的心灵及其局限性知之甚少，对教育环境也不太了解，更不清楚学校设置的各种课程的教育价值。他们选择科目的主要甚至唯一的标准就是这些科目有立竿见影的实用功能。在他们看来，学习一门现代语言的主要原因就是有利于商业交流，他们会清楚地表明他们的目的，至于达到目的的方法就留给教师的经验和判断了。对教育而言，和很多行为一样，最明显的方法很少是正确的，甚至可能带来灾难。不过，让注重实际的人参与教育管理有一个明显的好处，因为教师通常和商业界联系甚少，对商人的需求和想法也不太清楚，而这些人士则比较了解这些问题。教育局已经设立了一个教育家顾问委员会。为什么不设立一个类似的常委会，由国家商务委员会的代表参加？这个常委会对教育事业能够提出其他机构不能提出的宝贵意见。

从里柯克教授近期的一篇文章中，我们得知大约20多年前加拿大的中小学和大学发生了相当大的变化。"铁路巨头、公司经理、推销商、主管领导，还有各个行业的领头人，纷纷涌入大学，要求大学为他们的儿子提供实用的教育。"里柯克教授说，"有一所伟大而著名的公立学校，我曾经在那儿学习过，这所学校开始下定决心教授实用银行业务，金属格子、营业小窗口、用标签精确标注的账簿……银行用的形形色色的东西这里都有，看起来也很真实。但这些都结束了，在加拿大，他们现在开始认识到：最好的教育是让一个学生有开放的心灵。等时机到了，'你可以在银行里培训出一个银行家'。"可能不是每一个人都认识到了这一点，比如铁路巨头和其他有些人就还没有被完全说服，但里柯克教授

and all the rest of the group known as captains of industry, began to besiege the universities clamouring for practical training for their sons." Mr Leacock tells of a "great and famous Canadian public school," which he attended, at which practical banking was taught so resolutely that they had wire gratings and little wickets, books labelled with the utmost correctness, and all manner of real-looking things. It all came to an end, and now it appears that in Canada they are beginning to find that the great thing is to give a schoolboy a mind that will do anything; when the time comes "you will train your banker in a bank." It may be that everybody has not recognised this, and that the railroad magnates and the rest of them are not yet fully convinced; but Mr Leacock declares that the most successful schools of commerce will not now attempt to teach the mechanism of business, because "the solid, orthodox studies of the university programme, taken in suitable, selective groups, offer the most practical training in regard to intellectual equipment, that the world has yet devised."

To the same purport is the evidence given by Mr H.A. Roberts, Secretary of the Cambridge Appointments Board. The whole of this testimony deserves careful study. For some few years past the heads of the great business firms, in this country and abroad, have been applying in ever increasing numbers to Cambridge (and to Oxford also, though in this case statistics do not appear to be available) for men to take charge of departments and agencies; to become, in fact, "captains of industry." In the year before the war 1913-1914 about 135 men were transferred from Cambridge University to commercial posts through the agency of the Board. One might naturally suppose that the majority of these were science men; on the contrary, owing no doubt to the greater number of other posts open to them, they were fewer than might have been expected. Graduates from every Tripos are found in the 135 in numbers roughly proportional to the numbers in the various Tripos lists. Shortly before the war an advertisement of an important managership of some works—in South America, if I remember rightly—ended with the intimation that, other things being equal, preference would be given to a man who had taken a good degree in Classical Honours.

That most of such men are successful in their occupations might be deemed to be proved by the steady increase in the number of applications made for their

说最成功的商业学校现在不教商务运作了，因为"大学专业所提供的脚踏实地而正规的研究，是以挑选出来的合适群体为对象的，是目前智力发展的最实用的训练"。

剑桥职务委员会秘书罗伯特先生也发表过同样的意见。这个观点需要仔细研究。在过去的几年中，无论是国内还是国外的大公司领导，都不断增加在剑桥（当然也包括牛津，尽管在这方面好像没有统计数据）招聘的学生人数，任用他们来管理公司部门和代理机构，并把他们培养成了企业家。在战前的 1913~1914年。大约 135 人从剑桥大学毕业后，通过职务委员会相关机构推荐到了商业职位上。自然，有人认为这些人大部分都是理科生，考虑到他们有机会从事其他很多工作，这个人数的确比预期的人数少一些。在这 135人中，各个专业的人都有，和学校的专业比例差不多。战前，某个公司（大概是一个南美的公司，如果我没有记错的话）在招聘一个重要经理职位的广告中最后提出，其他条件等同的情况下，将优先招收有古典文学荣誉学位的人。

这些人在工作中大部分都很成功，这也可以从不断增加的招聘人数中得到证明。但是，还有更有力的证明。英国最大的公司之一向皇家委员会证明说，在过去 7 年公司招聘的 46 个剑桥学生中，有 43 个表现得很出色，两个人在试用期结束前跳槽选择了其他工作，只有一个不太让人满意。如果篇幅允许的话，还可以有很多证明。很清楚，在很多职业中，在任何程度上，一开始需要的不是技术知识，而是训练有素的头脑。

选择大学毕业生的另一个原因也很明显。赫肯先生

services. There is, however, more definite evidence available. A member of one of the largest business firms in the country testified to the same Royal Commission that of the 46 Cambridge men who had been taken into his employment during the previous seven years 43 had done excellently well, two had left before their probationary period was ended to take up other work; and one only had proved unsatisfactory. This evidence could easily be supplemented did space permit. It is clear, then, that in many callings what is wanted—to begin with, at any rate—is not so much technical knowledge as trained intelligence.

Another reason for thus choosing university men is not difficult to discover. When Mr W.L. Hichens (Chairman of Cammell, Laird and Co.) addressed the Incorporated Association of Headmasters in January last he declared that in choosing university graduates for business he looked out for the man who might have got a First in Greats or history, if he had worked—a man who had other interests as well, who was President of the Common Room, who had been pleasant in the Common Room, or on the river, or rowed in his college "Eight," or had done something else which showed that he could get on with his fellow-men. In business getting on means getting on with men.

The experience of Mr Hichens is so valuable that I cannot do better than quote further. "A big industrial organisation such as my firm, has, or should have three main sub-divisions—the manufacturing branch, the commercial branch, and the research or laboratory branch.... I will not deal with the rank and file, but with the better educated apprentices, who expect to rise to positions of responsibility. On the workshop side, we prefer that the lads should come to us between sixteen and seventeen, and, if possible (after serving an apprenticeship in the shops and drawing office), that they should then go to a university and take an engineering course.

"On the commercial side also we prefer to get the boys between sixteen and seventeen. We have recently, however, reserved a limited number of vacancies for university men. The research department also is, in the main, recruited from university men. But there is this difference, that, whereas the research men should have received a scientific training at the university we require no specialised education in the case

（卡米尔公司董事长）在去年一月校长联合会的会议上发言说，在挑选大学毕业生的时候，他会选择那些如果努力学习就可能会在古典文学或者历史上获得优秀成绩的学生，那些还有其他兴趣爱好的人，比如曾做过教师休息室的管理员，并干得很愉快，或者参加过赛艇队，或者做过其他活动，而且和同学相处融洽。在商业中，如何和人相处是非常重要的。

赫肯先生的经验极有价值，我最好再引用一段他的话："一个像我们公司这样的大机构，主要分为三个部门：生产部门、销售部门和研发部门……我不会和管理人员和文件打交道，而是和受过更好教育的学徒打交道，因为他们会晋升到重要的位置。在生产车间，我们希望年轻人十六七岁到我们公司，可能的话，在车间或者制图间当过一段学徒后，再进入大学学习工科。"

"在销售部门，同样我们也想要十六七岁的年轻人。但最近，我们还是为大学毕业生保留了几个位置。研发部门当然主要招收大学生。不同的是，研发部门的人员最好是理科专业，而对加入销售部门的人则没有专业方面的特别要求。学校里的专业化教育没有太多的实际价值，只要一个学生的大脑善于学习，在进入商业领域后有足够的时间来学习所有的技术知识。我们招收一个学生的时候，主要看他是否有能力和品性方面的长处，而且我认为教育的真正作用是教会一个学生如何学习和如何生活，而不是如何谋生。自然我们对一个学生是否有语言或者数学方面的才能很感兴趣，不过以学习语言为例，他到底是通过学习哪种语言——拉丁语、希腊语还是法语或德语——而具备的这种才能，则无关紧要了。教育价值至关重要，职业作用无足轻重。如果

of university men joining the commercial side. Specialised education at school is of no practical value. There is ample time after a boy has started business to acquire all the technical knowledge that his brain is capable of assimilating. What we want when we take a boy is to assure ourselves that he has ability and moral strength of character, and I submit that the true function of education is to teach him how to learn and how to live—not how to make a living. We are interested naturally to know that a boy has an aptitude for languages or mathematics, but it is immaterial to us whether he has acquired his aptitude, say for learning languages, through learning Latin and Greek or French and German. The educational value is paramount, the vocational negligible. If, therefore, modern languages are taught because they will be useful in later life, while Latin and Greek are omitted because they have no practical use, although their educational value may be greater, you will be bartering away the boy's rightful heritage of knowledge for a mess of pottage."

There are doubtless many different opinions as to the best way of training boys to become engineers, and in giving the results of his experience Mr Hichens does not claim that he is voicing the unanimous and well-considered judgments of the whole profession. His statement that "specialised education at school is of no practical value to us" would certainly be challenged by those schools which possess a strong, well-organised engineering side for their elder boys. But there would be substantial unanimity—begotten of long and often bitter experience—in favour of his plea that a sound general education up to the age of sixteen or seventeen at any rate, is an indispensable condition of satisfactory vocational training. "I venture to think," says Mr Hichens, "that the tendency of modern education is often in the wrong direction—that too little attention is given to the foundations which lie buried out of sight, below the ground, and too much to a showy superstructure. We pay too much heed to the parents who want an immediate return in kind on their money, and forget that education consists in tilling the ground and sowing the seed—forget, too, that the seed must grow of itself."

It would appear from what has already been said that though the necessity for vocational training exists in most, if not in all cases, the time in a boy's life at

学校教授现代语言是因为在以后的生活中有用，而不教拉丁语和希腊语是因为它们没有实际用处，虽说它们的教育意义更大，那你就是在教授知识上捡了芝麻丢了西瓜。"

哪种方法才是把学生培训成工程师的最佳方法？毫无疑问不同的人对此会有很多不同认识。谈到自己的经验时，赫肯先生没有断言他对这个职业的判断就是经过深思熟虑并为人们公认的。他认为"学校里的专业训练对我们来说没有太多实际价值"，这肯定也会遭到某些学校的质疑，这些学校对年长一些的学生有一套强有力而又精心编排的工科培训。但基于从长期而痛苦的经验中得到的共识，大家可能都会一致同意赫肯的请求，要想获得让人满意的职业培训效果，无论如何都应该在十六七岁之前对学生进行扎实的通识教育。他说："我甚至敢说，现代教育常常往错误的方向发展，我们太不注重基础了，因为基础的东西总是看不见的；我们过于注重那些显眼的上层建筑了。我们太重视父母的感受，他们总希望他们的投资有立竿见影的回报，因而忘记了教育是在耕地和播种，忘记了种子必须自己生长。"

如上所述，大部分情况下职业培训都是必要的，但是对不同的职业而言，学生开始培训的时间不同。即使大家对培训开始的一般年龄达成共识，例外情况或者学生能力的特殊性都可能导致其推迟，甚至推迟到一般人不能接受的年龄。因此，即使医学行业中表现最优秀的两个人分别以数学甲等和古典文学甲等成绩毕业，也并不能说明一般医学生也要等到23岁以后才开始接受职业训练。如果在某些领域年轻人必须接受

which such training ought to begin is far from being the same for all callings. Even where there is general agreement as to the normal age, exceptional circumstances or exceptional ability may justify the postponement of vocational instruction to a much later period than would usually be desirable. Thus the fact that two of the most distinguished members of the medical profession graduated as Senior Wrangler and Senior Classic respectively, will not justify the average medical student in waiting until he is twenty-three before commencing his professional training. If it be true that in some quarters "specialised education" has been demanded for young boys, it is equally true that many youths pass through school and enter the university without any clear idea of whither they are tending. This uncertainty may be due to a belief that "something is sure to turn up," to the magnitude of their allowances and the ease of their circumstances, occasionally, perhaps, to excessive timidity or underestimation of their powers; but, from whatever cause it springs, such an attitude of mind is deplorable in itself, and fraught with grave moral dangers. It ought to be possible in the case of a boy of sixteen or seventeen to say with some approach to certainty, for what employments he is quite unsuitable, and to indicate the general direction, at least, in which he should seek his life-work. The *onus* of choice is too often laid upon the boy himself; and the form in which the question is put—What would you *like* to be?—makes him the judge not only of his own desires and abilities, but also of the conditions of callings with which he can, at best, be but imperfectly acquainted. There is here fine scope for the co-operation of parents and teachers not only with each other but with the various professional and business organisations. It is generally supposed to be the duty of a head master to observe and study the boys committed to his care. It is equally important that he should extend that study and observation to their parents—as an act of justice to the boys, if for no other reason. But there are other reasons. There is knowledge to be gotten from every parent—or at least from every father—about his profession or business—knowledge which, as a rule, he is quite willing to impart. If, in addition, a head master avails himself of the opportunities of getting into touch with men of affairs, leaders of commerce, professional men of all kinds, his advice to parents as to suitable careers for their sons becomes

"专业教育"是事实的话，很多年轻人中学毕业后进入大学却并不清楚他们未来的方向，这同样是事实。这种不确定性可能源于一种想法——"某些变化总会发生"，可能源于津贴的多少、环境的变化，甚至也许源于他们过于害羞，或低估了自己的能力，但不论出于什么原因，这种态度本身就很可悲，充满了严重的道德风险。一个十六七岁的少年可以比较肯定地说出他不适合哪些工作，从而表明他会大致在哪个方向上从事其终身职业。选择的*重任*可能常常落在学生自己身上，并以这样的问题出现：你*想*成为什么样的人？这个问题让他不仅要考虑自己的能力和愿望，还要考虑他有可能从事的最好的但并不特别熟悉的职业的情况。在这方面，教师和父母有很好的合作空间，不但他们之间，还包括他们和不同的专业人士乃至商业机构之间的合作也有很大的空间。一个校长有责任细心观察和研究他的学生，同样重要的是，他应该把这种观察和研究延伸到学生父母身上，这种延伸如果没有其他原因的话，其目的主要是为了对学生公平。但事实上是有其他原因的。学生总会从父母至少是父亲身上学到他所从事的职业的知识，这也总是父亲们愿意交给子女的。如果一个校长有机会接触管理人士、商业领导、各种专业人士，那么他对于这些人的儿子更适合从事什么职业就能提出更有价值的建议。最起码，他可以使他们避免犯那些众所周知的错误，比如，他可以说服他们，看一个孩子是否适合学工科，不是说他能把自行车拆成零件，并渴望看"轮子滚动起来"就足够；一个学生擅长数字，也不能说明他就会成为一个好会计。简而言之，他不会让他们错误地把爱好发展成

enormously more valuable. At the very least he may save them from some of the more flagrant forms of error; for instance, he may convince them that there are other and more valuable indications of fitness for engineering than the ability to take a bicycle to pieces, and a desire "to see the wheels go round"; and that a boy who is "good at sums" will not, of necessity, make a good accountant. In short, he may prevent them from mistaking a hobby for a vocation.

It ought to be clearly stated that in writing of schools I have had in mind those which are usually known as public schools; for in the general preparation for practical life the public school boy enjoys many advantages which do not fall to the lot of his less-favoured brother in the elementary school. Not only does his education continue for some years longer, but it is conducted along broader lines, and gives him a greater variety of knowledge and a wider outlook. He comes, too, as a rule, from those classes of the community in which there are long standing traditions of discipline, culture, and what may be called the spirit of *noblesse oblige*. These traditions do not, of themselves, keep him from folly, idleness, or even vice; but they do help him to endure hardship, to submit to authority, to cultivate the corporate spirit, to maintain certain standards of schoolboy honour, and, as he himself would say, "to play the game." Though in the class-room it may be that appeals are largely made to individualism and selfishness, yet on the playing fields he learns something of the value of co-operation and the virtue of unselfishness. From the very first he begins to develop a sense of civic and collective responsibility, and, in his later years at school, he finds that as a prefect or monitor he has a direct share in the government of the community of which he is a member, and a direct responsibility for its welfare. Nor does this sense of corporate life die out when he leaves, for then the Old Boys' Association [①] claims him, and adds a new interest to the past, while maintaining the old inspiration for the future.

With the elementary school boy it is not so. To him, as to his parents, the primal curse is painfully real: work is the sole and not always effectual means of warding

---

① Old Boys' Association：老男孩联盟，此处指英国私立男校的校友会，其功能主要是促进本校毕业生之间的联系，募集校友捐款，资助学校建设等。

职业。

应该说清楚，在写到学校的时候，我心中想到的是公学，因为就对实际生活的一般准备而言，公学学生享有很多其他学校学生没有的好处。不仅仅是因为他们受教育的年头更长，而且他们的课程范围更广，这就赋予了他们更广泛的知识和更开阔的视野。一般而言，他所在的班级会有一些长期建立的传统，比如纪律、文化、位高则任重的精神，等等。这些传统本身可能不足以让他免于愚蠢、懒惰甚至邪恶等坏习惯，但足以帮他忍受困难、服从权威、培养合作精神、保持一个学生应有的尊严，以及就像他自己所说的一样"遵守游戏规则"。虽然在课堂上，他大多数情况下倾向于个人主义和自私自利，但在运动场上，他会体会到合作和无私的价值。一开始，他会慢慢培养出一种公民意识和集体责任感，后来，他会发现，作为年级长或者班长，他也是社区的一员，在社区管理中也有直接的一份，对社区福祉有直接的责任。即使他离开学校，这种合作意识也不会淡去，因为到了那时候，老男孩联盟就会召唤他，一方面激励他保持原有的对未来的期望，另一方面又增加他对过去新的兴趣。

对于一般的小学学生，情况则不同了。对他和他的父母而言，生活的原始诅咒既痛苦又真实：工作是他免于饿死的唯一方式，但这个方式却并不总是行之有效。他意识到他必须挣钱，只要法律允许，他甚至有可能被"变成钱"。作为家庭财政的贡献者，他在自己的王国里能有一定的声音来反对父母、上司或者国家侵害其自由的企图。事实上，在他开始工作的时候，大脑和身体都还没有成熟，训练也不足。几乎没有人教他合作精神；

off starvation. He realises that as soon as the law permits he is to be "turned into money" and must needs become a wage-earner. As a contributor to the family exchequer he claims a voice in his own government, and resists all the attempts of parents, masters, or the State itself to encroach upon his liberty. He begins work with both mind and body immature and ill-trained. There has been little to teach him *esprit de corps*; he has never felt the sobering influence of responsibility; the only discipline he has experienced is that of the class-room, for the O.T.C. and organised games are to him unknown; and when he leaves there is very rarely any Association of Old Boys to keep him in touch with his fellows or the school. Here and there voluntary organisations such as the Boy Scouts have done something—though little—to improve his lot; but, in the main, the evils are untouched. To find the remedy for them is not the least of the many great problems of the future.

The improvement of any one branch of industry ultimately means the improvement of those engaged therein. Scientific agriculture, for example, is hardly possible until we have scientific agriculturists. In like manner real success in practical life depends on the temper and character of the practitioner even more than upon his technical equipment. There are, however, three great obstacles to the progress of the nation as a whole, obstacles which can only be removed very gradually, and by the continuous action of many moral forces. We are far too little concerned with intellectual interests. "No nation, I imagine," says Mr Temple, "has ever gone so far as England in its neglect of and contempt for the intellect. If goodness of character means the capacity to serve our nation as useful citizens, it is unobtainable by any one who is content to let his mind slumber." Then again we suffer from the low ideal which leads us to worship success. From his earliest years a boy learns from his surroundings, if not by actual precept, to strive not so much to be something as somebody. The love of power rather than fame may be the "last infirmity of noble minds," but it is probably the first infirmity of many ignoble ones. Herein lies the justification of the criticism of a friendly alien. "You pride yourselves on your incorruptibility, and quite rightly; for in England there is probably less actual bribery by means of money than in any other

他对责任感也没有清醒的认识，唯一经历过的纪律就是在课堂上；他对军训和体育比赛也知之甚少；离开学校后，也没有老男孩这样的组织来帮他和学校或者同学保持联系。偶尔，志愿者组织——比如男童子军——会做点什么（虽说很少）来改变他的命运。但总体而言，他主要的命运还是不会有大的改变。如果能找到改善他处境的方法，则能帮助解决将来可能产生很多社会问题。

改进工业的任何一个分支，意味着最终改进所有相关的分支。比如，没有科学的农学家就没有科学的农业；同样，生活中真正的胜利取决于从业者的脾气和性格，而非技术设施。我们民族的进步有三大障碍，这三大障碍只能通过持续不断的道德努力来慢慢排除。首先，我们太不关心知识方面的兴趣爱好了。特波先生说："我想，没有一个国家像英国这样忽视和鄙视智力了。如果好的性格意味着可以成为一个有用的公民为国服务，但这个人的智力却没有得到开发，那么他也难以完成这个任务。"其次，我们没有远大的理想，以至于仅仅满足于成功。从很小的时候开始，即使没有确切的概念，一个男孩也能从周围环境中意识到，不费太多努力就能成为一个成功人士，获得某些成功。对权力而不是对名声的热爱可能是"高尚心灵最后的弱点"，但可能是很多不高尚的心灵最大的弱点。一个外国友人说得很好："你们英国人为你们的廉洁自律而骄傲，的确是这样，因为英国可能比世界上其他任何国家的金钱贿赂都少。*但你们所有人都可以用权力贿赂。*"最后一点（再用赫肯先生的话说）："太多的压力促使教育商业化，教育已经成了一门赚钱的生意，屈服于金钱，结果就把我们英国人变成了只关心赚钱的乌合之众。罗斯金曾经说过：没有一个

country. *But you can all be bribed by power.*" Lastly（to quote Mr Hichens yet once more）, "Strong pressure is being brought to bear to commercialise our education, to make it a paying proposition, to make it subservient to the God of Wealth and thus convert us into a money-making mob. Ruskin has said that no nation can last that has made a mob of itself. Above all a nation cannot last as a money-making mob. It cannot with impunity—it cannot with existence—go on despising literature, despising science, despising art, despising nature, despising compassion, and concentrating its soul on pence."

民族在自甘下贱之后，可以继续生存下去。当然，更没有一个自甘下贱、只关心赚钱的民族可以继续生存下去。没有一个民族可以在鄙视文学、鄙视科学、鄙视艺术、鄙视自然、鄙视宽容，而只把灵魂寄托在金钱上的情况下继续生存下去而不受惩罚。"

为了国家的福祉，肩负培育未来公民这一任务的人，必须从最能干的年轻人中选拔，必须让教师这个职业和其他职业一样，对年轻人具有吸引力。

——弗兰克·罗斯科

TEACHING AS A PROFESSION

By FRANK ROSCOE

Secretary of the Teachers Registration Council

The title of this chapter is prophetic rather than descriptive for although teachers often claim for their work a professional status and find their claim recognised by the common use of the phrase "teaching profession" yet it must be admitted that teachers do not form a true professional body. They include in their ranks instructors of all types, from the university professor to the private teacher or "professor" of music. Their terms of engagement and rate of remuneration exhibit every possible variety. Their fitness to undertake the work of teaching is not tested specifically, save in the case of certain classes of teachers in public elementary schools, nor is there any general agreement as to the proper nature and scope of such a test, could one be devised. Usually, it is true, the prospective employer demands evidence that the intending teacher has some knowledge of the subject he is to teach. He may seek to satisfy himself that the applicant has other desirable qualities, personal and physical, which will fit him to take an active and useful part in school work. These inquiries, however, will have little or no reference to his skill in teaching, apart from what is called discipline or form management.

The characteristics of a true profession are not easily defined, but it may be assumed that they include the existence of a body of scientific principles as the foundation of the work and the exercise of some measure of control by the profession itself in regard to the qualifications of those who seek to enter its ranks. Taken together, these two

论教师职业

弗兰克·罗斯科
教师注册委员会秘书

　　这篇文章的题目不是描述性的而是前瞻性的，因为教师虽然常常声称他们的工作很专业，并且通常使用"教师职业"来表明这一点，但还是必须承认教师还没有形成一个真正的职业群体。教师职业包括各种不同层次、不同类型，从大学教授到家庭老师、音乐导师。他们的参与度和报酬的不同也表明这个职业的多样性。除了公立小学某些班级外，教师是否适合相关岗位也没有专门的测试，即使设计了考试，这种考试的范围和性质是否合理也没有达成共识。通常，未来的雇主会要求有意向的老师对要教授的科目有一定的知识。如果申请人还有一些其他才能，无论是脑力方面还是体力方面的才能，雇主当然会更满意，这样可以让他在学校工作中更加积极和有用。这些要求，除了对所谓的纪律和形式管理有用之外，对他的教育技能没有任何参考。

　　一种真正职业的特点是不太容易定义的，但也许可以认为，这些特点应该包括，有系统的科学的原理作为这项职业的基础，同时职业本身有一些控制措施，来审

characteristics may be said to mark off a true profession from a business or trade. The skilled craftsman or artisan may belong to a union which seeks to control the entrance to its ranks, but the difference between the member of the Amalgamated Society of Engineers and the member of the Institution of Mechanical Engineers is that the former belongs to a body chiefly concerned with the application of certain methods while the latter belongs to one which is concerned with those methods, not only in their application but also in their origin and development. It is recognised that there is a body of scientific knowledge underlying the practice of engineering, and the various professional institutions of engineers seek to extend this knowledge, while claiming also the right to ascertain the qualifications of those who desire to become members of their profession. The same is true in different ways with regard to the professions of law and medicine. It is to be noted also that within these professions the admitted member is on a footing of equality with all his colleagues save only so far as his professional skill and eminence entitle him to special consideration.

It will be seen at once that there are great difficulties to be overcome before teaching can be truly described as a profession. The diversity of the work is so great that it may be held that teaching is not one calling but a blend of many. It is difficult to find any common link between the university professor, the head master of a great public school, an instructor in physical training, and a kindergarten teacher. It is not easy to bring together the head master of a preparatory school, working in complete independence, and the head master of a public elementary school, dealing with pupils of about the same age as those in the preparatory school, but controlled and directed by an elected public authority under the general supervision of the Board of Education. Yet despite these apparent divergences of aim all teachers may be regarded as pursuing the same end. They are engaged in bringing to bear upon their pupils certain formal and purposeful influences with the object of enabling them to play their part in the business of life. Such formal influences are seconded by countless informal ones. School and university alone do not make the complete man and it is an important part of the teacher's task to second his direct and purposeful teaching by the influence of his own personality and conduct, and by securing that the form or school

查那些要进入这个职业的人员的资格。放在一起的话，这两个特点可以表明这是一种职业，而非一种商业或行业。熟练的手工艺人或艺术家可能属于一个协会，这个协会的目的就是控制进入这个行业的人员的数量。工程师联合会成员和机械工程师协会成员之间的不同在于：前者主要考虑的是对某些方式的运用，后者主要考虑的不仅是这些方式的运用，还包括这些方式是如何产生和发展的。大家都认识到，工程实践中有很多潜在的科学知识，不同的工程师协会都在设法拓展这些知识，并保证自己有权利来确认那些想加入这个行业的人有足够的资质。对于法律和医学行业也一样，只是方式不同而已。还应该注意到，在这些行业中，已经认可的成员之间地位是平等的，除非某个人的专业技能和名声赋予他特殊的待遇。

很快就能发现，教师要真正被看作一种职业，还有很大的困难需要克服。这个工作是如此多样化，以至于可以说教书不是一种工作，而是多种工作的混合。要在大学教授、公学校长、体育老师和幼儿园老师之间找到一个共同点几乎是不可能的。要把一个预备小学的校长和一个公立小学的校长协调到一起也是不太容易的，因为预备小学的校长工作完全独立，而公立小学的校长虽然管理的是同样年龄的学生，其工作却必须由一个选举出来的公共权威人士指导和管理并接受教育局的一般监管。不过，虽然在目标上有明显的分歧，但所有的老师可能都在追求同一个结果。他们都想带给学生正规而目的明确的教育，使他们能在以后的生活中做出自己的贡献。这些正规的影响后面还有无数不正规的影响。中小学和大学本身并不能造就一个完整的人，教师要完成自

is in harmony with the general aim of his work.

Skill in imparting instruction is by no means the whole of the equipment required by a teacher. It is indeed possible to give "a good lesson" or a series of "good lessons" and yet to fail in the real work of teaching. In some branches far too much stress has been laid on the more purely technical and mechanical attributes of good teaching as distinct from the finer and more permanent qualities such as intellectual stimulus, the awakening of a spirit of inquiry, and the development of a true corporate sense. By way of excuse it may be said that teaching has tended to become a form of drill chiefly in those schools where the classes have been too large to permit of anything better than rigid discipline and a constant attention to the learning of facts. Teachers in such circumstances are gravely handicapped in all the more enduring and important parts of their work. Very large schools and classes of an unwieldy size tend to turn the teacher into a mere drill sergeant.

While full provision should always be made for the exercise of the teacher's individuality there must be sought some unifying principle in all forms of teaching work. Unless it is agreed that the imparting of instruction demands special skill as distinct from knowledge of the subject-matter we shall be driven to accept the view that the teacher, as such, deserves no more consideration than any casual worker. No claim to rank as a profession can be maintained on behalf of teachers if it is held that their work may be undertaken with no more preparation than is involved in the study of the subject or subjects they purpose to teach. A true profession implies a "mystery" or at least an art or craft and some knowledge of this would seem to be essential for teachers if they are to have professional status.

The difficulty in this connection is that the principles of teaching have not yet been worked out satisfactorily. Our knowledge of the operations of the mind develops very slowly and those who carry out investigations in this field of research are few in number. Their conclusions are not necessarily related to teaching practice but cover a wider field. The study of applied psychology with special reference to the work of the teacher needs to be encouraged since it will serve to enlarge that body of scientific principle which should form the basis of teaching work. It is by

己的任务，还需要靠自身行为和人格的影响来协助直接的教学，并保证学校的教学和自己的目标保持一致。

传授知识肯定不是一个教师应该具有的全部技能。一个老师，很有可能上了一堂"好课"或一系列的"好课"，但在真正的教学上却还是不成功。在有些教学中，大家过于关注技术和设备方面的因素，而忽略了如何培养学生更优秀、更持久的才能，比如智力开发、质疑能力、团队精神等。有些人可能会找借口说，教学已经变成了一种训练，主要因为有些学校班级太大了，只能要求刻板的纪律和不断的学习。在这种情况下，老师们受到很大的限制，难以从事那些更重要和更持久的工作。过大的学校和班级好像把老师变成了训练官。

在尽力培养教师个性的同时，教学工作也应该有一个统一的原则。除非大家都同意，传授知识需要特殊的技能，完全不同于学科知识本身，否则我们就不得不接受这样一个观点，做一个教师和随随便便做一个工人一样简单。如果有人说教师工作可以不经过太多准备，把需要教授的课程学习一下就可以了，那这些人没有站在教师的角度，把教师当作一种职业。一种真正的职业意味着一种"神秘性"，或者至少是一门艺术，了解了这些知识对一个教师而言非常重要，这样他们才能有专业地位。

这方面的困难在于，教学原则还没有完全研究出来。在大脑运作机制方面，我们的知识进展很缓慢，在这个领域开展研究的人也很少。他们的研究结果不但和教学实践相关联，还会覆盖更广泛的领域。应用心理学研究，尤其是和教师工作相关的部分应该加以

no means necessary, or even desirable, that teachers should be expected to spend their time in psychological research. Their business is to teach and this requires that they should devote themselves to applying in practice the truths ascertained and verified by the psychologists. For this purpose it will be necessary that they should know something of the method by which these truths are sought and proved. It is also an advantage for teachers to learn something of the history of education, not as a series of biographies of so-called Great Educators but rather with the object of learning what has been suggested and attempted in former times. Such a knowledge furnishes the teacher with the necessary power to deal with new proposals and with the many "systems" and "methods" which are continually arising. Instead of becoming an eager advocate of every novelty or adopting an attitude of indiscriminate scepticism he will be in some measure able to estimate the true merit of new proposals, and his knowledge of mental operations will serve as an aid in judging whether they have any germ of sound principle. The alternative plan of leaving the teacher to learn his craft solely by practice often has the result of confining him too closely to narrow and stereotyped methods, based either on the imperfect recollection of his own schooldays, or on the method of some other teacher. Imitation is cramping and serves to destroy the qualities of initiative and adaptability which are indispensable to success in teaching.

It will be noted that no extravagant demand is put forward on behalf of what is called training in teaching. The methods of training hitherto practised have been based too frequently on the assumption that it is possible to fashion a teacher from the outside, as it were, by causing him to attend lectures on psychology and teaching method and to hear a course of demonstration lessons. This plan may fail completely since it is possible to write excellent examination answers on the subjects named and even to give a prepared lesson reasonably well without being fitted to undertake the charge of a form. It should be recognised that the practice of teaching can be acquired only in the class-room under conditions which are normal and therefore entirely different from those existing in the practising school of a training college. When this truth is fully apprehended we may expect to find that the young teacher is required to spend his first year in a school where the head master and one or more members of the

鼓励，因为这可以扩大具有科学原则的群体，有助于形成教学工作的基础。而教师本身则没有必要把时间花在心理研究上，这可能也没有多少益处。他们的工作是教学，应该主要投身于把心理学家验证了的真理应用于实践。为了这个目的，他们也有必要了解一些寻求和证明这些真理的方法。同样有益的是，教师也应该学习一些教育历史，不是学习那些所谓伟大的教育家的生平，而是学习教育在历史上所获得的成果。这样的知识，能让教师有能力应对教学中不断产生的新提议和不断出现的许多"体系"和"方式"。这样，他们不会急切地支持任何一种新的东西，也不会采取一种不加辨别的怀疑主义。他们会在一定程度上有能力去评估新的提议真正的优劣，而在心理机制方面的知识则可以帮助他们判断这些新的提议是否源于坚实的理论原则。另一种方法，即仅仅让老师通过实践学习教学方法，常常会把他们局限于狭隘陈旧的教学方式，这些方式可能是他们的老师用过的方法，或者是其他老师教学方法的零散记忆，模仿只会束缚并破坏开创精神和因材施教的方法，而这两者正是教学成功不可或缺的因素。

在教育训练方面，大家还没有提出太过分的要求。但目前所实施的方法基本源于这样一种假设：可以通过听心理学和教学法讲座，以及听示范课这些外部培训培养一个老师。这个计划可能会完全失败，因为一个人有可能为某些规定科目的考试做出精准的答案，或者把一堂准备过的课上好，却并不适合承担教师的责任。必须认识到，教学实践只能在正常的课堂条件下获得，这些条件和培训学校的情况完全不同。如果充分认识到了这

regular staff are qualified to guide his early efforts and to establish the necessary link between his knowledge of theory and his requirements in practice.

The Departments of Education in the universities should be encouraged to develop systematic research into the principles of teaching and should be in close touch with the schools in which teachers are receiving their practical training.

The plan suggested will be free from the reproach often levelled against the existing method of training teachers, namely, that it is too theoretical and produces people who can talk glibly about education without being able to manage a class. It will also recognise the truth that the young teacher has much to learn in regard to the art or craft of teaching and that there are certain general principles which he must know and follow if he is to be successful in his chosen work. The application of these principles to his own circumstances is a matter of practice, for in teaching, as in any other art, the element of personality far outweighs in its importance any matter of formal technique or special method. The ascertained and accepted principles underlying all teaching should be known and thereafter the teacher should develop his own method, reflecting in his practice the bent of his mind.

The recognition of a principle does not of necessity involve uniformity in practice. Freedom in execution is possible only within the limits of an art. The problem is to define these limits in such a liberal manner as will allow for variety and individual expression. The saying that teachers are born, not made, is one which may be made of those who practise any art, but the poet or painter can exercise his innate gifts only within certain limits and with regard to certain rules. It is no less fatal to his art for him to abandon all rules than it is for him to accept every rule slavishly and apply it to himself without intelligence.

The acceptance of the principle that there is an art or at least a craft of teaching is a condition precedent to any attempt to make teaching a profession in reality as well as in name.

The further requirement is that those who are engaged in teaching should have some power of controlling the conditions under which they work and more especially of testing the qualifications of those who desire to join their ranks. This demands a

一点，我们希望年轻老师在学校的第一年中，可以由校长和一两个正式教师指导他们最初的实践，以便帮助他们把理论知识和实践联系起来。

大学的教育系应该积极开展教学原理方面的研究，并和进行教师实训的学校保持密切联系。

目前培训老师的方法太理论化了，只会让培训出的人谈论起教育滔滔不绝，在实践中却连一个班都管理不了，我们这个提议旨在解决这个问题，因此可能不会受到大家的批评。另外必须认识的一个真理是，就教学艺术而言，年轻老师有很多要学习的东西，如果他们想在工作中获得成功，有一些一般原则要学习和遵守。把这些原则运用到自身的情况中是一种实践，因为在教学中，就像在任何其他艺术中一样，人格因素的重要性远远压倒其他技术或特殊方法的重要性。在学习了大家广为接受和广泛证明过的一般教学原理后，一名教师还应该通过实践，开发出一套适合自己特点的教学方法。

承认一个原理并不意味着在实践中一成不变地运用这个原理。一门艺术在自身的领域内可以自由地运用，问题在于如何开明地界定艺术的范畴，以便允许多样而有个性的表达。有关老师是天生的而非后天培养的说法，可能是某些从事艺术的人说的，但诗人和画家也必须在某些限制和规则下发挥自己的天赋。抛弃所有的原则，和盲目而不动脑筋地遵守每一项原则，对艺术同样是致命的。

如果要承认教育在现实中和在名义上都是一种职业，首先必须接受的一个原则就是：教育是一门艺术。

将来的要求可能是，从事教师职业的人，必须有

recognition of the essential unity of all teaching work and a consequent effort to bring all teachers together as members of one body, possessing a certain unity or solidarity in spite of its apparent diversities. To form such a body is a task of great difficulty since the various types of teachers have in the past tended to separate themselves into groups, each having its own association and machinery for the protection of its own interests. Apart from the teaching staffs of the various universities, there are in England and Wales over fifty associations of teachers, ranging from the National Union of Teachers with over ninety thousand subscribing members to bodies numbering only a few score adherents. These associations reflect the great diversity of teaching work already described, but all alike are seeking to promote freedom for the teacher in his work and to advance professional objects. Such aspirations have been in the minds of teachers for many years and from time to time attempts have been made to realise them by establishing a professional Council with its necessary adjunct of a Register of qualified persons. Seventy years ago the College of Preceptors, with its grades of Associate, Licentiate and Fellow, suggesting a comparison with the College of Physicians, was established with the object of "raising the standard of the profession by providing a guarantee of fitness and respectability." The College Register was to contain the names of all those who were qualified to conduct schools, and admission to the Register was controlled by the College itself in order to provide a means of excluding all who were likely to bring discredit upon the calling of a teacher by reason of their inefficiency or misconduct. The scheme thus launched was, however, not comprehensive, since it concerned chiefly the teachers who conducted private schools and did not contemplate the inclusion of those who were engaged in universities, public schools, or the elementary schools working under the then recently established scheme of State grants. Teachers in schools of this last description were apparently intended by the government of the day to be regarded as civil servants, appointed and paid by the State. Subsequent legislation modified this arrangement, but teachers in schools receiving government grants are still subject to a measure of control, and those in public elementary schools are licensed by the State before being allowed to teach. It will be seen that the effort to organise a teaching profession was

能力来掌控他们的工作环境，尤其是要有能力来测试申请进入这个行业的人员的资质。这就要求教师要认识到所有教学工作具有基本的一致性，并随后努力把所有教师团结在一个集体之中，虽然大家工作各不相同，却能团结一致。要形成这样一个集体是很困难的。因为在过去，不同类型的老师往往组成不同的团体，每一个团体都有自己的组织和方式来保护自己的利益。除了不同大学的教职员工外，从超过 9 万名会员的全国教师联合会，到只有几十个支持者的小组织，在英格兰和威尔士还有 50 多个教师团体组织。这些组织反映了教师职业极其多样。不过所有的组织都致力于提高教师在工作中的自由度，推进职业目标。教师们多年来就有这些想法了，大家时不时通过建立专业委员会来为合格人员注册以实现这些想法。70 年前的师范学院将教师根据不同等级分为副教授、执业者和院士，提出可以和医学院一样确定职业目标，并把其目标定位为："保障健康和尊严，提高职业标准。"学院注册部门计划登记所有有资格教书的教师的名字，注册本身由学校自己负责，这样可以避免把那些因为能力不足或行为不端而给教师职业抹黑的人注册进来。这个计划并没有广泛地开展，因为计划主要包括在私立学校教书的老师，而没有仔细考虑是否应该把按照国家规定运作的大学、公立学校和小学的老师包括在内。后面谈到的这一类老师，很明显被政府看作公务人员，由国家任命和发薪水。虽说后来的法律更改了这一类教师的身份，但接受政府资助的学校里的教师仍然受到国家控制，而公立小学的教师教书之前要由国家颁布证书。可以看出，教师职业从一开始就有一个障碍，

hampered from the start by the fact that teachers were not entirely free to set up their own conditions, since the State had already taken charge of one branch, while further difficulties arose from the varied character of different forms of teaching work and from the circumstance that some of these forms were traditionally associated with membership of another profession, that of a clergyman.

Hence it was that despite several attempts to institute a Register of Teachers and to organise a profession the difficulties seemed to be insurmountable. Between the years 1869 and 1899 several bills were introduced in Parliament with the object of setting up a Register of Teachers but all met with opposition and were abandoned. The Board of Education Act of 1899 gave powers for constituting by Order in Council a Consultative Committee to advise the Board on any matter referred to the Committee and also to frame, with the approval of the Board, regulations for a Register of Teachers. It was not until 1902 that an Order in Council established a Registration Council and laid down regulations for the institution of a Register. The Council thus established consisted of twelve members, six of whom were nominated by the President of the Board of Education [1] while one was elected by each of the following bodies: the Headmasters' Conference, the Headmasters' Association, the Head Mistresses' Association, the College of Preceptors, the Teachers' Guild, and the National Union of Teachers. The members of the Council were to hold office for three years, and afterwards, on 1 April, 1905, the constitution of the Council was to be revised. The duty assigned to the Council was that of establishing and keeping a Register of Teachers in accordance with the regulations framed by the Consultative Committee and approved by the Board of Education. Subject to the approval of the Board the Council was empowered to appoint officers and to pay them. The income was to be provided by fees for registration and the accounts were to be audited and published annually by the Board to whom the Council was also required to submit a report of its proceedings once a year.

Under this scheme a Register was set up, with two columns, A and B. In the former

---

[1]   Board of Education：一般指学校董事会、地方教育局。此处指英国教育部，现在改为 Department for Education。

即教师不可能完全自由地来安排他们的工作环境，因为国家已经控制了一部分。其他的困难则来自不同种类的教师工作特点的不同。另外，现在有些教师的工作从传统上就和另一个职业——牧师的一部分工作联系在了一起。

因此，除了几次建立教师注册机构的尝试，要承认教师是一个职业，看起来好像困难重重。在 1869 到 1899 年之间，有几个法案被递交给国会，希望建立一个教师注册机构，但都遭到反对，最后没有通过。直到 1899 年通过的教育部法案，获权根据法律建立一个顾问委员会来为教育部就相关事务提供建议，并经教育部的批准制定教师注册机构的规章制度。1902 年，由议会同意建立注册委员会，并制定了注册机构的规章制度。注册委员会由 12 名成员构成，其中 6 名由教育部部长任命，其他由下列组织各选举一人：校长会议、校长联合会、女教师委员会、师范大学、教师行会和全国教师委员会，注册委员会成员任期 3 年。1905 年 4 月 1 日，委员会的规章制度进行了修改。委员会的职责是根据顾问委员会制定、教育部同意的规章制度，设立教师注册机构并保障其运行。经过教育部的同意，注册委员会有权任命官员并支付其薪酬。委员会的收入主要来自注册费，其账户由教育部审查并每年公布一次。注册委员会每年还需向教育部提交一次工作报告。

在这种规划下，注册表制定出来了，包括 A、B 两栏。A 栏是所有在公立小学获得国家证书的教师的名字。这不需要教师申请或者支付任何费用，而是自动注册。B 栏是为中学教师保留的，包括私立中学和公立中学。这

were placed the names of all teachers who had obtained the government certificate as teachers in public elementary schools. This involved no application or payment by such teachers, who were thus registered automatically. Column B was reserved for teachers in secondary schools, public and private. Registration in these cases was voluntary and demanded the payment of a registration fee of one guinea in addition to evidence of acceptable qualification in regard to academic standing and professional training. Although teachers of experience were admitted on easier terms the regulations were intended to ensure that, after a given date, everybody who was accepted for registration should have passed satisfactorily through a course of training in teaching. As designed in the first instance Column B furnished no place for teachers of special subjects and it became necessary to institute supplemental Registers in regard to music and other branches which had come to form part of the ordinary curriculum of a secondary school.

The scheme thus provided a Register divided into groups according to the nature of the accepted applicant's work. Such an arrangement presented many difficulties since it ignored all university teachers and assigned the others to different categories depending in some instances on the type of school in which they chanced to be working and in others on the subject which they happened to be teaching.

A professional Register constructed on these lines had the seeming advantage of supplying information as to the type of work for which the individual teacher was best fitted. On the other hand it was held that the division of teachers into categories was unsound in principle and the teachers in public elementary schools were not slow to resent the suggestion that they belonged to an inferior rank and were properly to be excused the payment of a fee. They pointed out that many of their number held academic qualifications which were higher than those required to secure admission to Column B wherein some eleven thousand teachers had been registered, of whom not more than one half were graduates. The views thus expressed were shared by many other teachers and it speedily became manifest that the proposed Register could not succeed. In the Annual Report of 1905 the Council stated that under existing conditions it was not practicable to frame and publish an alphabetical Register of

种注册是自愿的，要求提供学术和专业训练方面的合格证明，并交纳1几尼（旧时英国金币，合21先令。译者注。）注册费。虽说有经验的老师更容易获得承认，但这个规定的目的是在某个日期之后，每一个获得注册的老师都已经学过教师培训课程，并且通过了这方面的考试。正如最初设计的一样，B栏后面没有地方留给特殊课程的老师了。考虑到音乐和其他中学日常教学课程，有必要进行补充注册。

补充注册计划根据注册申请者的工作性质把注册分为不同的组。这种安排，因为没有包括所有大学教师，同时在给其他教师分类的时候，有时候是根据教师正好所在的学校的类型，其他时候则是基于他们正在教授的学科，结果带来了很多困难。

在这种方针下设计的专业注册表，看起来好像有利于提供每个教师最适合哪种类型的工作方面的信息，但从另一方面来看，把教师分成不同类型基本上不合适，而且公立小学的教师很快就不满了，认为这种分类好像暗示他们低人一等，连注册费都不用缴纳。他们指出，公立小学的很多教师在学术方面的资历甚至超过了有些在B栏注册的人。而B栏大概有11000人注册，其中大学毕业生还不到一半。这种说法得到了很多教师的认同。事实很快表明这种注册方式很难成功。委员会1905年的年度报告指出，在当时的情况下，要按照1899年法案提出的原则制定和公布一个按教师姓氏字母排序的注册表，是不大可能的。1906年6月，教育部公布了一个备忘录，解释了为什么要利用即将通过的法律所提供的机会来废除注册，1906的教育法案也补充了一个条款，说明为什么要取消顾问委

Teachers such as appeared to be contemplated in the Act of 1899. In June, 1906, the Board of Education published a memorandum stating the reasons which had led it to take the opportunity afforded by impending legislation to abolish the Register, and in the Education Bill of 1906 a clause was inserted which removed from the Consultative Committee the obligation to frame a Register of Teachers. This clause was strongly opposed by many associations of teachers. It was urged by these bodies that although one scheme had failed yet a Register was still possible and desirable. It was held by many that the task assigned to the Registration Council had been an impossible one since the conditions of supervision and control imposed under the Act of 1899 left the Council very little freedom and wholly precluded the establishment of a self-governing profession. The general opinion seemed to be that any future Register must be in one column avoiding any attempt to divide those registered into different classes and that any future Council must be as independent and widely representative as possible. This opinion found expression and official sanction in a memorandum issued by the Board of Education in 1911 after several conferences had been held for the purpose of promoting a new registration scheme. The memorandum stated that: "It should not be so much the kinds of teachers likely to be most rapidly or easily admitted to the Register that should specially determine the composition of the Council but rather the larger and more general conception of the unification of the Teaching Profession." This new and wider idea served to govern the formation of the Teachers Registration Council which was established by an Order in Council of February, 1912. The body constituted by this Order consists wholly of teachers and includes eleven representatives of each of the following classes: the Teaching Staffs of Universities, the Associations of Teachers in Public Elementary Schools, the Associations of Teachers in Secondary Schools, and the Associations of Teachers of Specialist Subjects. The Council thus numbers forty-four and it is ordered that the chairman shall be elected by the Council from outside its own body. At least one woman must be elected by each appointing body which sends more than one representative to the Council provided that the body includes women among its members. It will be seen that the constitution aimed at forming a Council wholly

员会建立教师注册机构的规定，这个条款受到了很多教师组织的反对。很多团体指出，虽然前一个计划失败了，但注册还是可能完成并带来好处的。他们认为，这个任务正是因为安排给了注册委员会，所以难以完成，因为 1899 年通过的法案对委员会有严格的监管和控制，使其只有很少的自由，并完全阻止了建立一个自治行业的可能性。因此，将来的任何注册都只能有一栏，从而避免把注册的教师分成不同等级，将来的任何注册委员会也必须越独立、越具有广泛的代表性越好。教育部为此召开了几次会议商讨建立新的注册机制，这个意见写入了 1911 年的备忘录并得到了官方批准。备忘录指出："不应该太快和太轻易地承认教师有那么多种类，应该特别注意注册委员会的构成，对教师职业应该有一个更统一、更宽泛的概念。"在这个包容的新想法的指导下，根据 1912 年 2 月教师指导委员会的一个法案，新的教师注册委员会成立了。这个机构的成员全部都是教师，以下四类组织每一类 11 个代表：大学教师协会、公立小学教师协会、中学教师联合会、特殊科目教师联合会。因此新的注册委员会有 44 个成员，规定主席要从委员会以外的人中选举。为了保证女性成员的人数，规定每个选送代表超过两个的组织，如果其成员中有女性的话，必须至少要有一个女性代表。可以看出，这个机制的目的是建立一个完全独立、最具广泛代表性的委员会。这个目标通过 10 个委员会的建立进一步得到保障，这 10 个委员会代表了不同形式的特殊教育，并提出任何委员会制定的注册条件，在公布前必须提交给这些委员会批准。

根据这些规划，第一届注册委员会于 1912 年成立，

independent and thoroughly representative. This quality was further ensured by the establishment of ten committees, representing various forms of specialist teaching and providing that any conditions of registration framed by the Council should be submitted to these committees before publication.

The first Council under this scheme was formed in 1912 and held office for three years as prescribed by the Order in Council. The chairman was the Right Honourable A.H. Dyke Acland and the members included the Vice-Chancellors of several universities and representatives of forty-two associations of teachers. The first duty of the Council was to devise conditions of registration and these were framed during 1913, being published at the end of that year. They provide in the first place that up to the end of 1920 any teacher may be admitted to registration who produces evidence of having taught under circumstances approved by the Council for a minimum period of five years. Regard for existing interests led to the setting up of a period of grace before the full conditions of registration came into force. After 1920, however, these become more stringent and require that before being admitted to registration the teacher shall produce evidence of knowledge and experience, while all save university teachers are also required to have undertaken a course of training in teaching. Under both the temporary and later arrangement the minimum age for registration is twenty-five and the fee is a single payment of one guinea. There is no annual subscription.

The second Council was elected in 1915 and appointed as its chairman Dr Michael E. Sadler, Vice-Chancellor of the University of Leeds. Up to the middle of July, 1916, the number of teachers admitted to the Register was 17,628 and the names of these were included in the *Official List of Registered Teachers* issued by the Council at the beginning of 1917. The Register itself is too voluminous for publication since it comprises all the particulars which an accepted applicant has submitted. All registered teachers receive a copy of their own register entry together with a certificate of registration. It will be seen that the task of receiving and considering applications for registration forms an important part of the Council's work. But it is by no means its chief function. As is shown in the Board of Education memorandum already quoted the Council is intended to promote the unification of the teaching profession. The

并根据议会法案运行了三年。主席是阿克蓝德阁下，成员包括几所大学的副校长和42个教师协会的代表。委员会的第一项职责是规定注册条件，这些条件于1913年制定，并在年底公布。注册条件首先提出，到1920年底，任何教师只要在注册委员会认可的情况下，提供最少5年教学实践的证明，都可以获批注册。考虑到某些利益，注册条件完全实施前有一段缓冲期。在1920年以后，注册条件会严格执行，所有教师都必须提供知识和经验方面的证明，并要求除了大学教师以外的所有教师在注册前，都必须接受教师培训课程。在当时和以后，最小注册年龄都是25岁，注册费一次性缴纳1几尼，没有年费。

第二届注册委员会是1915年选举的，任命利兹大学副校长麦克赛德隆为主席。到1916年7月中旬，注册的教师是17628名，这些教师的名字登记在1917年初委员会公布的《注册教师官方名单》中。注册名单太长了，页数太多了，以至于没有出版，因为名单包括了注册教师提供的所有详细信息。所有注册教师都得到一份个人注册名单副本和注册证书。可以看出，接受和考查注册申请已经成了委员会工作很重要的一部分，但绝非其主要功能。正如教育部指出的那样，成立注册委员会是为了促进教师职业的统一性。注册只是这种统一性的象征，委员会还负责一项重要工作，即就教师工作各方面的问题，从一个团体的角度来表达教师的意见。这从教育部部长在委员会第一次会议上的发言就可以看出来。在对委员会成员表示欢迎后，他补充道："委员会的目标不仅仅是完成教师注册。委员们在教师职业的很多其他领域和方面都能起作用。我希

Register is nothing more than the symbol of this unity and the Council is charged with the important task of expressing the views of teachers as a body on all matters concerning their work. This is shown in the speech made by the Minister of Education at the first meeting of the Council. After welcoming the members he added:

"The object of the Council would be not only the formation of a Register of Teachers. There were many other spheres and fields of usefulness for a Council representative of the Teaching Profession. He hoped that they would be able to speak with one voice as representing the Teaching Profession, and that the Board would be able to consult with them. So long as he was head of the Board they would always be most anxious to co-operate with the Council and would attach due weight to their views. He hoped that they on their side would realise some of the Board's difficulties and that the atmosphere of friendly relationship which he trusted had already been established would continue."

The functions of the Council are thus seen to extend beyond the mere compilation of a Register of Teachers and to include constant co-operation with those engaged in educational administration. In view of the desire which is now generally expressed for a closer union between the directive and executive elements in all branches of industry it is safe to assume that the Teachers' Council will grow steadily in importance, especially if it is seen to have the support of all teachers.

Meanwhile it furnishes the framework of a possible teaching profession and gives promise of securing for the teacher a definite status by establishing a standard of attainment and qualification. More than this will be required, however, if the work of teaching is to be placed on its proper level in public esteem. Those who undertake the work must be led to look for something more than material gain. The teacher needs a sense of vocation no less than the clergyman or doctor. It has been said that "teaching is the noblest of professions but the sorriest of trades" and the absence of any real enthusiasm for the work inevitably produces an attitude of mind which is alien to the spirit of a real teacher. The material reward of the teacher has accurately reflected the want of public esteem attaching to his work. For the most part a meagre pittance has been all that he could anticipate and this has led to a steady decline in the number

望委员们在代表教师这个职业的时候，能用一个声音说话，教育部能从你们那儿得到参考意见。只要我还是教育部的领导，我们将很乐意和注册委员会合作，并对你们的意见给予足够的重视。我希望你们能认识到教育部也有很多困难，但这两个组织已经建立的友好关系必将持续下去。"

注册委员会的功能不限于编辑《注册教师》，还包括和其他教育管理机构的合作。人们期望在教育部门的指导机构和执行机构之间建立更紧密的联系，因此可以设想，在所有教师的支持下，教师委员会的重要性会不断增加。

同时，委员会制定了教育职业的框架，承诺通过建立教师资质和学识方面的标准来保障教师的地位。要保证教师工作受到公众的尊敬，得到应用的地位，要做的还有很多。承担教育工作的人，要认识到有比物质收获更重要的东西。教师和牧师、医生一样，需要职业成就感。人们常说："教师是最高尚的工作，最可怜的行业。"如果对这项工作缺乏真正的热情，只会导致一种和真正的教师精神格格不入的态度。对教师的物质奖励准确地反映了公众对这项工作的尊重。大部分情况下，教师只能期待微薄的收入，而这导致入行人数不断下降。一项职业应该保障从业人员有相应的前途并确保其成员获得尊重。而在教师职业中，这些机会都很少，自然也很难吸引足够多的能干和有抱负的年轻人。解决的方法是对那些证明了他们是优秀教师的人，让他们有机会进入教育工作和教育管理的每个部门。

为了国家的福祉，肩负培育未来公民这一任务的

of recruits. A profession should furnish a reasonable prospect of a career and a fair chance of gaining distinction. Such opportunities have been far too few in teaching to attract able and ambitious young men in adequate number. The remedy is to open every branch of educational work and administration to those who have proved themselves to be efficient teachers.

The national welfare demands that those who are to be charged with the task of training future citizens should be drawn from the most able of our young people, to whom teaching should offer a career not less attractive than other callings. In particular the teacher should be regarded as a member of a profession and trusted to carry out his duties in a responsible manner. Excessive supervision and inspection will tend to discourage and eventually destroy that quality of initiative which is indispensable in all teaching. Freed from the monetary cares which now oppress him, definitely established as a member of a profession having some voice in its own concerns, encouraged to exercise his art under conditions of the greatest possible freedom, and provided with reasonable opportunity for advancement, the teacher will be able to take up his work in a new spirit. We may then demand from new-comers a sense of vocation and expect with some justification that teachers will be able to avoid the professional groove which is hardly to be escaped and which is quite inevitable if the conditions of one's work preclude opportunity for maintaining freshness of mind and a variety of personal interest. Such limitations as accompany inadequate salaries, lack of prospects and absence of professional status convert teaching into "a dull mechanic art" and deprive it of its chief elements of enjoyment, namely the free exercise of personality and the recurring satisfaction of seeing minds develop under instruction, so that we are conscious of our part in helping the future citizens to make the most of their lives. It is this power of impressing one's own personality on the pliable mind of youth which brings at once the greatest responsibility and the highest reward to the teacher and attaches to his task a true professional character since it may not be undertaken fittingly by any who cherish low aims or despise their work.

人，必须从最能干的年轻人中选拔，必须让教师这个职业和其他职业一样，对年轻人具有吸引力。教师也应当成为一种被认可的职业，要相信教师会负责任地履行职责。过度的监管和检查只会削弱甚至破坏教师的创新能力，而创新能力对教师职业是不可或缺的。如果让教师有足够的收入，不再为金钱而苦恼；如果教师真正成为一个职业，能够发出自己的声音；如果教师能在最自由的情况下发挥他们的教学艺术；如果教师有进步和晋升的合理机会，那么教师们会以一种全新的精神来从事他们的工作。然后，我们就可以希望新成员有职业成就感，并有理由希望教师们可以避免职业低谷。如果一个人的工作环境不能让他保持心灵的新鲜度和个人兴趣的多样化，职业低谷常常是不可避免的。这方面的限制，加上薪水不足、没有前途、不受大众认可，使教师工作成为一种"枯燥而机械的艺术"，剥夺了其让人享受的主要因素，即在自由培养学生的个性和指导学生心灵的成长中获得满足感，并在这个过程中意识到教师是如何帮助未来的公民把生活变得更有意义的。正是这种用自己的性格来影响年轻人可塑心灵的权利，为教师职业赋予了最大的责任感和最高的奖赏，赋予了教师职业一种真正的专业性。因为任何鄙视自身工作的人，任何缺乏远大目标的人都不适合承担这项工作。